Acclaim for Sta

The Rescue

When Jesus Shows Up
and Transforms Your Pack

"As a songwriter, I am driven by a passion for the power of a story. My friend Stacey and her husband Johnny share that same passion and have been voices of hope reaching millions of people through the radio waves over the years. I am so excited for this new book and the stories it holds. I believe these heartfelt words Stacey has written will lead you to discover how God is at work in your own story, and remind you that no story is too hopeless to be rescued by your Savior."

— Matthew West
Singer/Songwriter

"There is nothing more powerful than a life that has been radically transformed by the power of God's intentional love. Daily, I hear such stories on my national radio program, Intentional Living, but no story more moving than Stacey's. In her new book, Stacey Stone will take you along on her personal journey as she faces the reality of the loss that she has suffered and how she was rescued. Take a few moments, grab your favorite coffee or tea and breathe in the knowledge that you are part of The Rescued Breed as well."

— Dr. Randy Carlson
Founder of Intentional Living and
President of Family Life Communications

"Stacey Stone is well known as a great communicator and personality from her radio days. Little did we know just how doggone funny she is! Stacey weaves together spiritual truths and simple life lessons with "tales" from man's (and woman's) best friend. The Rescued Breed will put a smile on your face and give you something profound and meaty to chew on!"

— MARK GILROY
Publishing Veteran and Author of the
Kristen Conner Mystery Series

"I love the word transformation. It's a word of hope, potential and life for each of us. In her book The Rescued Breed, Stacey Stone brings the word transformation to life as she allows us to be a part of her journey with her dog Bogey. I'm a dog person, so she had me hooked at the introduction of Bogey. Then I quickly discovered that the insight, wisdom and hope that Stacey shared was captivating and life changing for me, indeed, transformational. I encourage you to take this journey with Stacey and Bogey. As you do you will too will quickly discover that God will use the insight Stacey shares in these pages to touch and transform you in a very special way. You will be glad you did."

— JEFF LOVE
Lead Teaching Pastor at Alive Church,
Tucson, AZ

"Stacey Stone fills your heart with hope and joy in this incredible story of Christ's unending love. "The Rescued Breed: When Jesus Shows Up and Transforms Your Pack" reminds you that God can be seen in all things, big and small, and sometimes in the most unlikely places, even in a little dog."

— BETSY BUCK
Actor and On-Air Talent

"Through the eyes of Stacey and her dog Bogey I came to see more clearly the eyes of God and His love for me. You will too. Some books you read and others you feel. I really felt this one. You will too. This book is a love story between a woman and a dog, a woman and her husband and beyond these between a woman and her God. Read it and become a part of the story."

— ROB CRUVER
Senior Pastor at Zarephath Christian
Church, Zarephath, NJ

"The moment you meet Stacey - you know there is something different about her. She brings an energy, an optimism and a wise perspective with her whenever she walks into a room. But it only takes a few moments with her to learn where that something special comes from - it comes from her relationship with Jesus. From years of walking with Him and trusting in Him - through the good times and the tough times, she and her husband Johnny are a blessing. So - take time to engage her book and let some of her energy, optimism and faith rub off on you!"

— KERRICK THOMAS
Pastor of The Journey Church – Manhattan,
New York, New York

"Stacey and Johnny show us how to share our faith while trusting God. Others talk about how to share their faith, The Stones actually do it in this book, that you will not be able to put down. You will be encouraged by these candid stories no matter where you are in your life."

— ROBERT TAYLOR
General Manager, The Bridge Christian Radio,
New Jersey

The Rescued Breed

When Jesus Shows Up and Transforms Your Pack

Stay Blessed,
Stacey!

STACEY STONE

with JOHNNY STONE

Copyright © 2015 Johnny and Stacey Stone
Stone Studios, LLC
All rights reserved.

ISBN-13: 978-1515378310
ISBN-10: 1515378314

Scripture quotations are taken from
The Holy Bible, English Standard Version® (ESV®).
Copyright © 2001 by Crossway, a publishing ministry of
Good News Publishers. All rights reserved.

Cover art and interior design copyright © 2015 by Pamela Pachmayr
"Today" photographs copyright © 2015 by Pachmayr Studios
Pamela Pachmayr Creations, LLC. All rights reserved.
Pamela@PachmayrStudios.com, www.PachmayrStudios.com

All rights reserved. No part of this book may be reproduced or
transmitted in any form without permission in writing from the author.
Contact the author at Stacey@TheRescuedBreed.com

Dedication

For Madison, Benjamin, Peyton, Cameron and Hannah;

in case you need to know how awesome Jesus is
and I'm not here to tell you.

Contents

A NOTE FROM STACEY

*O*ne afternoon I had an appointment at my church in Manhattan, so I took the train from Jersey into Penn Station. Once there, I found myself on a loading dock between Penn Station and Madison Square Garden. As many times as I had taken this trip into the city, I had never ended up in this place. I took off walking because I was going to be late, walking between big trucks and the men working on them towards the sunlight.

When I emerged onto the street, I was at a taxi stand I had never seen before. (After seven years, I thought I had seen them all!) It was a little disconcerting and as I walked up to the taxi concierge, he asked me if I needed a cab. "Yes, indeed!" I replied, and he led me to the second cab in line, stating that the first driver simply wasn't paying attention. As it turns out, there wasn't anything simple about it. It was part of God's plan. The concierge opened the door to the cab and looked me straight in the eye, exclaiming, "You are going places!"

I sat back in the cab for a moment and smiled because I was going places—to my church's office to talk with the pastors about teaching during our services at Journey Church Manhattan on Sundays. I was feeling excited about teaching, pleased with my pleasant encounters during my personal journey so far that morning, and blessed by God. But God wasn't done yet.

The cabbie smiled at me and asked me where I was headed. I gave him the address of the church. He asked for it again. Because of my Texas accent, I was sure I was talking too fast, so I slowed down and repeated the address. Looking puzzled, he said that he knew the street pretty well and didn't recognize that address. I explained it was my church's office and that I was on my way to a meeting. He asked what type of church it was, so I explained that we were Christ-followers and told him all about Journey Manhattan. He said he was Muslim, and then asked me an unexpected question: When someone does something wrong, do we bring them before the church and punish them? I laughed and said no, because we would then be too busy to do anything else! I told him that we believed in God's grace shown to us in Jesus Christ, and in trying to live as close to His way as possible.

Our conversation continued during the entire ride and when he said that Jesus was not the Son of God, I told him he was wrong and the Bible and history proves it over and over. By now we were sitting in front of the church offices and I was going to be late for my meeting, but I still felt that God was not done. The taxi driver asked me about Mary and the virgin birth and ended with asking if he would be welcome at my church. I told him to come anytime, and we would welcome him with open arms. He dropped his head and said quietly, "You would not be welcome at my church."

I happened (by God's perfect timing, not coincidence) to be holding on my lap a copy of David Nasser's book Glory Revealed, which I was taking to one of my girlfriends in the church office. (If you have not read David's book, his Iranian family is Muslim and severely chastised him when he became a Christian. It's an amazing story, and I definitely recommend it!) I encouraged my driver to start reading the Bible and gave him David Nasser's book. I also agreed to read the portion of the Koran about Mary.

When I got out of that New York City cab, I could not stop smiling! My heart was full of joy. That day proved two things to me: Jesus was in that cab with us, and a book can change a life. Do I know if the cab driver read the book? No, but I would bet my life that he did. Did he give his life over to Christ? Not in that moment, but Jesus was after him, and I don't doubt Jesus for a second.

I pray someday that someone finds this book in his or her lap and that Jesus has his way with it. And that's why I will take the time and put in the effort to write this book for you. God has placed this book into your hands for a reason. A book can change a life.

In these pages I want to share what I have learned over the years about surviving loss, change, anxiety and life in general with Christ. Yes, it's the account of my wonderful dog, Bogey, but it's also about my radio career and so much more. It's a story of hope that captures the happy moments when I truly realized I wasn't alone. It's a collection of moments about the transformation that God orchestrated in my life and with my pack. Transformation that only He can bring.

Now allow me to share the story of how a little dog rescued me, and how Jesus has rescued us all.

A Separation for Now...

It was a cold, winter day.

Isn't that how a lot of stories start out – with wind whipping through the trees and ominous clouds on the horizon? This story starts the same way, but also on a couch in front of a warm fireplace with a little dog curled up next to me. It sounds perfect but at that moment, the dog that saved my life was in the process of losing hers. She didn't fully understand why I cried for hours on end as we sat there together, comforting each other for the last time...

I can't fully understand how the world will go on when Bogey will leave me here, sitting alone, within the hour. Our appointment with the vet is at 3:20. Everyone says that putting her to sleep is the ultimate humane act of love, one that will end her pain. One minute I want to pick her up from her pillow and run as far away as I can and the next minute, I cry and accept that we have to go through with this.

Why don't we have hospice for dogs? I've done this before with a human, my grandmother, and the hospice nurses were so helpful and kind and knowing. The morphine I gave my beloved Grandmommie was a stepping stone to pain free living but they also made us understand that it was a path to death. Now, I will have to verbally tell the vet to take this dog's life.

What will the minute after that feel like? In 45 minutes I will know.

Grief is a funny thing. Okay, not funny "ha-ha" but funny "strange" – because it is one of the few moments that bring all of your achievements and successes in life into clarity of perspective. Being in this moment, with Bogey taking her last breaths beside me, I would trade all of it for tomorrow.

Grief also has a way of taking your outer shell and crushing it with the weight of your tears. Being totally exposed, your loss creates a feeling of emptiness in your chest and the atmosphere of walking around with your skin totally removed. She's not gone yet and I feel this weight – how will I stand upright when she will be dead in 32 minutes.

I want to scream at God, *NO!* But He gave me this beautiful gift – I didn't find her, she found me – so I can't be angry about how she has to die. Seventeen years ago on a cold winter day in the exact same month as now, she rushed to me for help and my life was never the same. She has never left my side until 28 minutes from now.

The TV is off and all we can hear is the crackling fire as I tell her the stories of our lives. I remind her there were moments when it was she and I, period. There was no one else in our world for those moments and she rescued me from myself. I laugh and she looks up with joy at the sound. She's ready, but I am not and have no choice as the moments slip away.

I want to feel her heartbeat. It's a fluttering little sound and when she stops breathing, it stops too. My wish is that she would be wrapped in love at home when she goes but the illness is too slow and too cruel to take her. She starts breathing again and I feel her heartbeat once again against my chest. Guilt for the disappointment that she did not pass sweeps over me and the clock starts ticking again. 14 minutes.

Bogey is snoring now and I am thinking about all of the things this little rescue dog has taught me. All of the life lessons that her love has shown me and I have to tell someone else who can benefit from that love. Are you that person? If you are reading this, I pray you are. She changed my life forever but more than anything she helped me understand that I was rescued, too.

It is time.

Even though I walk through
the valley of the shadow of death,
I will fear no evil, for you are with me;
your rod and your staff, they comfort me.

PSALM 23:4

DON'T BE AFRAID
TO JUMP IN SOMEONE'S LAP

(Accept the Joy That Comes Into Your Life)

I put my hand in the pocket of my jacket one crisp fall morning and came out with handfuls of used tissues. I'm talking roughly an entire box worth, holding so many tears that no one could ever count. I started laughing at the sight of me standing there with tissues falling all over the floor and filling both of my hands. My husband, Johnny, called up from downstairs wanting to know if I had finally lost it. "No, I was just cleaning out my coat pockets," I replied.

Even though I was laughing through my tears, I realized there was much more to that moment. The last time I had worn that jacket, I was grieving. Grieving a big part of my life, a gift of joy I let into my heart the day 17 years earlier when I visited the golf course. Finding those tissues and laughing like that meant I had finally moved to the stage when I could feel joy again.

Sometimes you create your joy and sometimes it darts in unexpectedly like the rainy day my first husband and I went to the golf course. Golf courses are not my favorite places on earth. They are pretty to look at in the summertime but I have never played and never had any desire to play. Anyway, small town Texas had put in a new, PGA level golf course and the plan was just to drive through.

Well, anyone who knows me knows that I can't just drive through many places because of my teeny, tiny bladder. Every trip, every stop has to include a nice, clean restroom that I can enjoy for a few minutes. This trip was no different so we pulled up as close to the restroom as possible and I got out in the miserable rain. As I ran towards the ladies room door, I noticed a little black flash running up at the same time. When I opened the door, the flash ran inside. The heat inside the restroom hit my face at that exact moment and I said, "So, it's not me you want to meet. It's the heat in here!"

This precious little canine face looked up at me from its drenched, muddy coat and we both agreed in that moment that, if nothing else, I was going to let her stay in the warmth. Neither of us knew then the warmth she brought would stay in my heart forever.

I sat down (not too much detail here) and she ran under the stall door and jumped right into my lap. Surprised, I didn't react until she had burrowed her little muddy head up into the side of my neck. She was shivering and wet so I pulled her back to look at her more closely and promised her that we would try and figure out who she belonged to.

A swift trip to the Pro Shop told us that she was not one of theirs and that dogs were abandoned all the time at that resort. The guys gave her a polo shirt with their golf course logo on it so she could be wrapped up and off we went to put an ad in the paper to see if she had been lost.

No one answered the ad. I would love to say that I took her home and never looked back but I offered that dog to my grandmother, my mother-in-law, friends and **anyone** else I thought might need some companionship. At the time, I already had two dogs but this new one wasn't going anywhere.

She already had a name (Bogey – named after the golf shot and not the actor!) so she moved right in.

If I had not been open to that sweet, muddy face and all that love and joy, I would have missed 17 beautiful years with Bogey. If I had been too busy to stop and take the time to recognize her need, she would have loved the next woman to come through that door or the next one after that. Even before I knew I needed her, **God knew**. Matthew 6:33 promises us that God gives us what we need before we know we need it: *But seek first the kingdom of God and his righteousness, and all these things will be added to you.*

Don't think for one second that I was Super-Christian during this time. I would not have been nominated for any awards during those days but I was serving in the church and doing the normal things someone who enjoys church will do. I sang in the choir and served along with my mother at various functions. I was even Rudolph in a Christmas program one year so I guess that was part of what He wanted me to do, red nose and all (okay, maybe I should've gotten an award for that one).

I wish I could say I felt like I deserved the level of love God was giving me but my self-esteem would never allow that admission to pass my lips. Having dedicated my life to Christ at the age of seven, I came in and out of what was supposed to be the greatest love of all on my part too. But God knew that someday I would lay it all down at His feet and deserve that little dog's love.

You could say that I was too busy for love. Six months after Bogey met me at that bathroom door, I also started my radio career. Twelve hour days, weekends, holidays, little salary; radio is not the most glamorous career you can choose if you want there also to be room for serving Christ. He would eventually make it so I could serve Him each day in my job but that took 10 years because of my stubbornness. Wanting to do things my way, I pushed love and service to the side to achieve great things in my career.

But each night when I returned home, Bogey was there reminding me that her gift of love was non-negotiable and given straight from God. My wish for you is that you open your heart to what joy God has planned for you. If you are going to discover how to follow what God has put into your heart you have to let Him in. Jesus says, *Behold, I stand at the door and knock. If anyone hears my voice and opens the door, I will come in to him and eat with him, and he with me* (Revelation 3:20).

I also want you to consider letting God heal your heart. Maybe you've pushed the pain down further and further until you're stifled by the past and can't love or find joy again. *The Lord is near to the brokenhearted and saves the crushed in spirit.* (Psalm 34:18). He doesn't want you to go through life like that, He wants you to rest in His open arms and be free. King David understood your pain and wrote, *I will run in the way of your commandments when you enlarge my heart!* (Psalm 119:32).

> **He doesn't want you to go through life like that, He wants you to rest in His open arms and be free.**

Start your journey of joy with opportunities that are right in front of you. One early morning, Johnny and I were getting ready for the day and he simply started singing the "Ma-Na-Ma-Na" song from Sesame Street. I answered back with the funny second line and off we went, full of the happy memories of watching Sesame Street during our childhoods. That one moment of silliness with my husband stayed with me the rest of the day because I was keeping that joy alive.

So, what do you love to do? What makes you smile the minute you think about it? And what do you excel at? Those are the simple things with which you can start to invite joy into your life.

My trip to the golf course that day in 1993 brought me the stories in this book, some filled with joy and some with great sorrow. But most of all it helped me realize that even in difficult times, there are great days ahead when we are open to the joy God wants to give us.

In this you rejoice, though now for a little while,
if necessary, you have been grieved by various trials.

1 Peter 1:6

Johnny

I don't remember the first time I met Bogey.

I do, however, remember the first time I heard Bogey. She only barked for two things: other dogs on the TV and when Stacey got on the phone. This was back when we only had land lines and it never failed that when I was calling Stacey about the show or later when we were dating, Bogey would let loose with this irritating bark that just screamed "Pay attention to me!" In fact, one year for Stacey's birthday I wrote and recorded a song all about her love for the makeup counter and how I was going to eat Bogey in a hot dog bun someday.

Actually, now that I think about it, I do remember the first day that I met Bogey simply because it was a radio station event. At Young Country 105.3 we put on an event called "Weiner Dog Races" and Stacey thought it would be a good idea to bring Bogey.

You did notice that I said that Bogey liked to bark at other dogs on TV, right?

Well, Bogey must have thought that she was watching TV because she barked at the other dogs the entire time. Stacey finally had to take her home because she was disrupting the races with the other dogs barking back at her. Not a brilliant way to make my acquaintance!

In some ways, though, it feels like Bogey has always been part of my life…

LICKING SALTY TEARS

(The Great Fade)

irports represent the "great fade" for me. If you are standing at the airport, the planes fade from view, and if you are on the plane, the airport fades from view. I have lived several pivotal moments of great fades, both from the airport and from the airplane.

One of those moments was in 2000 with Bogey in my lap in the airport as my first husband boarded his plane. It was prior to 9/11, so no one stopped us from going to the gate together and saying goodbye. Everyone who loves loses at some point. It may be that the love was never meant to be, or that it is simply the wrong time of your life. It can be one-sided or a mutual realization that life has different paths for each of you to take. Regardless of the many reasons, that's where I found myself that day at O'Hare Airport.

We had discussed and fought our way through his visit, and I was about to be left alone in Chicago with my little dog. All of my life's expectations converged and said good-bye on that day, as the husband whose love I'd been in the process of losing boarded a plane and left me sitting there. The past walked down the jetway and took off like a shot, rising higher and higher until it could no longer be seen.

My tears flowed as the realization of what was to come sank into my heart. Bogey tried to lick my salty tears off my neck as I strained to find the will to get up and walk away from the gate and go on with another day. Then a song came to me that captured the moment and, with people rushing all around us trying to get somewhere, I started to sing to my little dog:

> You and me against the world,
> sometimes it feels like you and me against the world.
> When all the others turn their backs and walk away,
> I can count on you to stay.
> And when one of us is gone,
> and one of us is left to carry on,
> then remembering will have to do.
> Our memories alone will get us through.
> Think about the days of me and you,
> you and me against the world.[1]

I sang that same song to Bogey on the day that she died, ending the slow fade of her death. It's amazing to me, looking back, that I was blessed with the companionship of this little dog for 17 years. Through all the fades of those years, she was right by my side.

I really had no idea that airports and "great fades" would be such a huge part of my life. Broadcasting was my passion and loving Jesus was my life, so it seemed like the perfect match to put the two together. But the steps leading up to that airport heartbreak and my Chicago adventure were so ordained that I couldn't fathom the life-altering experience I was about to have.

Before I moved to Chicago, I had been fired twice, resigned once and altogether left radio for public relations in order to

---

1   *You and Me Against the World* Kenny Ascher and Paul Williams

get a paycheck. Not a wise move. Never run after money—do what you love and the money will take care of itself. So I started praying that God would show me the path I was supposed to be on. Another piece of advice here: if you ask God to open doors, you are supposed to walk through them and let God shut the doors you are not supposed to enter. Get ready for the sound of slamming doors!

Then the offer came to co-host a morning show in Chicago and we knew it was the right opportunity for me. It was a very, very ripe time in my life for what God's will was and for my will bending to His. They offered me more money than I had ever worked for and I would be serving God at the same time but it meant moving to Chicago before my first husband could follow. In other words, I was about to be alone with my little dog.

After eight years in broadcasting and thirty-four years of life in Dallas/Fort Worth, I boarded a plane to Chicago on Mother's Day. I will never live down the fact that I left my mother on Mother's Day, but that was how it worked out, so off I went. My mother and father took me to the airport and Bogey and I said our good-byes. Through my sobs, I placed her under the seat in front of me and prepared for take-off on this new adventure.

Little did I know that my luggage was taking its own adventure! My parents were crying and watching as the luggage was loaded onto the plane. As one of the trams came around a corner, they watched as my suitcase flew off and the tram kept going! Always taking care of me in one way or another, my father started beating on the glass as my mother ran over to the counter. The crew eventually came back and retrieved my suitcase.

Hours later, I arrived at a hotel in Elk Grove Village, Illinois, with God's plan for my life, *two* suitcases, and a little dog. It had always been a dream of mine to live in a hotel where someone else makes your bed and they feed you every night, but after sixty days of hotel living, I learned to never, ever wish for something like that again! The excitement of a new place to live was overshadowed by the sadness of being alone, no family to fall back on, and a morning run-in with a skunk (more on that in Chapter 4).

That same day, I also began listening to God's unique plan for my life as never before. But there was one thing missing from this exciting adventure: my first husband. He had stayed behind in Texas, with the plan that he would move to Chicago once we knew the job was what we thought and everything was settled.

I married him, my college sweetheart, on the exact same weekend he graduated. Looking at the two of us from the outside, you would have assumed that we'd be married forever. We were really great friends, both wanted the same things, brought up in the church, college graduates, and both sets of our parents were still married at that time. The researchers would have agreed with you.

But even with the odds ever in our favor, neither of us was prepared to put any work into our marriage. The sad truth is we put a lot more work into our wedding than we did our marriage. We were great as friends, but not so great as husband and wife. I'm sorry to say that we had never been taught to make each other top priority. At first, I was busy getting my Master's degree and he was busy working. He worked nights, and I was gone during the day, so we were a lot like passing ships.

Then he started to play golf on the weekends, and I would go shopping with my family or, later on, go to work on Saturday. We started going to church separately, and most of the time his was "The Church of the Eighteen Holes." I thought we might be in trouble when I started actually encouraging him to play *more* golf. I moved away for my dream job and for a year I flew back one weekend a month to see him, but if I was being honest it was mostly to see my family. One week he did not return my phone calls so I called his close friend, who said he was just really busy. I asked him to have my husband call me because I was really worried.

When I arrived at the airport in Texas that weekend, I called and left a message for my husband to call me back because we obviously needed to talk about what was going on. He did, we met and agreed to a divorce. He drew up the divorce papers, went to the courthouse without me, and our marriage was over.

That story encompasses thirteen years of my life and the slowest fade of a marriage I have ever seen. I would love for every woman contemplating marriage to learn from my mistakes and not have to go through what I have been through, but I know that can't happen. Upon marrying, my life goals and dreams should have included being the best wife possible. I was also not very good at leaving my father and mother and putting my husband first. That's what the Bible teaches, but I was too busy striving for my career goals to work on my marriage. The striving part also took its toll on my Christian integrity as I pushed to get ahead rather  **You have to decide what or who is most important in your life and protect those relationships first.**

than seeking to follow God's leading. You have to decide what or who is most important in your life and protect those relationships first.

The slow fade was over and God began to heal and prepare me for a new beginning that would surpass my wildest imagination of the love He had planned.

Behold, I am doing a new thing;
now it springs forth,
do you not perceive it?
I will make a way in the wilderness
and rivers in the desert.

Isaiah 43:19

3

Barking Up the Wrong Tree

(You Will Make Mistakes and Have Regrets)

There I was, Little Miss Independent, just me and Bogey in the big, windy city of Chicago. My very first snowfall there was 17 inches, and everyone was walking around saying, "This is nothin'! I remember when it was 85 below zero and you couldn't expose your skin or it would crack off!" I thought you could walk on top of a big snow bank (what did I know?) so I placed Bogey on top of a pile of snow during our first walk in the snow. She fell through, threw her head back, and stared at me, with those eyes of hers asking, "What have you done now?"

I am actually quite proud that both Bogey and I survived our time in Chicago. The horror stories can wait for now, but the one time I tried to cut Bogey's nails cannot because I am sharing about making mistakes and this one was huge!

Being a woman on my own, I decided that I needed to learn to care for my dog myself, not running to the groomer each time she needed her nails trimmed. Brushing Bogey's teeth was never an option (hence her twelve lost teeth, but I still have ten fingers), but the nail trim seemed like a good idea at the time. So I deemed one Saturday "Spa Day" for Bogey. I gave her a bath, dried her fur and her paws, and even cleaned out her ears. Then came time for the nail clipping (insert ominous music here). For this part I had purchased a special tool for trimming a dog's nails. I sat down in the recliner with Bogey on her back on top of me and cut one nail. Just one nail! And the blood started spurting everywhere! I had never seen that much blood! I couldn't get it to stop. It bled and bled, and after thirty minutes I called the vet in a panic.

The nice lady on the other end of the phone suggested that I get some flour out of the cabinet and put her foot in it to stop the bleeding. Seemed like a good idea, but she didn't realize she was talking to a single woman in a panic who did not have any flour in her house. I grabbed the closest thing I had – Bisquick – and stuck Bogey's paw into a bowlful. Bogey screamed a sound that I had never before heard come from a dog! She wanted to get as far away from me and that bowl of Bisquick as she possibly could. I jerked that box off the counter and read the ingredients only to discover that Bisquick contains **salt** as well as flour. So Bogey was screaming and crying, and I was crying, and there was Bisquick all over both of us, and we were one, big, huge mess!

No one lives a perfect life. Just like I was never the perfect dog owner, you can never be the perfect daughter, son, husband, wife, employee, and so on. You will have your regrets. The wonderful thing is that people will love you anyway, even when you are not perfect. And certain people in your life will "get you" and understand you (though not always) and love you absolutely, no matter what. These people are showing you what it means to be loved by God.

As flawed as we are, God loves us and shows us how to love one another. First John talks about this kind of love. This letter by the apostle John explains in depth how God's love works among us: *Beloved, let us love one another, for love is from God, and whoever loves has been born of God and knows God. Anyone who does not love does not know God, because God is love. In this the love of God was made manifest among us, that God sent his only Son into the world, so that we might live through him. In this is love, not that we have loved God but that he loved us and sent his Son to be the propitiation for our sins. Beloved, if God so loved us, we also ought to love one another. No one has ever seen God; if we love one another, God abides in us and his love is perfected in us* (1 John 4:7-12).

Do you think God didn't know the mistakes you were going to make in your life before He sent Jesus to save us all? Wrong! He knew I was going to pick up that box of Bisquick and stick Bogey's foot in it. God knows we are going to make mistakes, and He loves us anyway. First John 3:20 specifically spells it out: *For whenever our heart condemns us, God is greater than our heart, and he knows everything.* He knows what you've done in the past and still loves you. He knows what you will do in the future and still wants to love you.

Do you think God didn't know the mistakes you were going to make in your life before He sent Jesus to save us all?

Bogey forgave me. I washed off her foot and cried some more. When I think about it, I still cry a little, but I know that she forgave me. Her little brain probably forgot about it that same day, but I still beat myself up about my need for independence and not just paying to have her nails clipped. But God knows my heart, and He and Bogey are both laughing at me as I remember what I did and tears come to my eyes again. God loves me no matter what. Bogey loved me no matter what, too. **I'm** the one who needs to learn to love and forgive myself.

Why do we hang on to our regrets for so long? I once had a very wise person tell me that regret does nothing good for us unless we use it to change something for the better. I never put Bogey's paw in Bisquick again, so I did learn from my regret. Bogey was very glad for that!

I also learned—very quickly—not to trust Bogey around

goose poop, or regret would take on a whole new meaning. Growing up in Texas, I did not realize that Canada geese are poop factories. Every park I have visited in the Midwest and Northeast is filled with the geese's little green presents that can ruin an otherwise wonderful day. I took Bogey to a company picnic once (pets were welcome), but I wasn't watching her closely enough, so she proceeded to roll, on her back, in goose poop. Then she jumped in my unsuspecting lap! My picnic ended really quickly, and I learned to watch for the goose poop whenever I had Bogey with me in a park.

That was a relatively small, amusing regret from which I learned a small lesson. Most all of us have bigger, more serious regrets as well. There were times in my life when I was selfish or didn't think before I acted, times that I deeply regret now. Can I go back and change them? No. Have I learned from them? I hope. Do I carry them around like baggage? It depends on which day you ask me.

I learned one more very valuable lesson about regret from my grandmother. For one year, I took time off from my career to care for my grandmother while she was in assisted living. Since Bogey was a huge joy for her and the other people at the home, I had Bogey certified and approved to visit in my grandmother's circle of care. When I talk about the circle of care that the elderly receive, I'm referring to the emergency room that leads to a hospital room that leads to rehabilitation and then back to assisted living. I became a pro at helping my grandmother around this circle, and even handling the countless changes in prescriptions that caused me to pull my hair out on a regular basis.

One day in the rehab where my grandmother would go after a hospital stay, I was giving her a manicure and a pedicure. She was relaxing on her bed, enjoying being pampered, when I noticed that she had started to cry. Whoa! What were the tears about? My 83-year-old grandmother looked me in the eye and said that she wished she had done things like this for her mother when her mother was in the nursing home.

Whoa again! Let me tell you what my grandmother did for her mother, my great-grandmother, when she was in the nursing home. My grandmother, Katheryn Baldwin Hatcher, basically gave up her life to take care of her mother. She would work long hours at the railroad, scheduling shipments, and then would trade out with my Uncle Bubby, her brother Vance, every other night visiting Maggie, their mother. That included doing her laundry, having dinner with her, and making sure she was getting her medications and proper care. They did everything that caregivers do to serve the one they love, no matter where in the circle of care, until that loved one moves on to Heaven.

That's what my grandmother did. Did she give her a mani and pedi? I guess not. But she did give her mother the care that she needed when a brain tumor the size of a grapefruit moved in and took over. That qualifies in my book as doing all that you can do, and I told her so that day.

But my grandmother still had her regrets. As I told her about how I stuck Bogey's foot into a bowl of Bisquick, we laughed through our tears. I heard several stories that day about how my grandmother cared for her mother. I told her the mantra I carry in my head and heart now: "No Regrets!" But I fear she carried her regrets to her grave. I don't want to do that, and I don't want you to either. God loves us and forgives us, and our regret suggests that we must also forgive ourselves.

For every time I was not the greatest pet owner – no regrets! Every time I was not the greatest daughter – no regrets! And for every time I was not the greatest wife – no regrets! Today is the only day that you get, period, so no regrets. The Bible says, *So teach us to number our days that we may get a heart of wisdom* (Psalm 90:12). You will make mistakes. Let them carry you to the loving and forgiving arms of God. It's hard to let go of big regrets, hard to forgive ourselves. But we can't redo life. We can only use our past mistakes to lead us into a better future. Carrying regrets around with us weighs us down and is a mistake. Carry them to the foot of the cross of Jesus and leave them there.

> *For whenever our heart condemns us, God is greater*
> *than our heart, and he knows everything.*
>
> 1 JOHN 3:20

4

LEARNING TO HEEL

(Be There for Someone Else)

Johnny Stone and I had known each other and even worked together in some capacity, off and on, for many years. I started as an intern on his Texas morning show on KYNG, Young Country. A few weeks after he landed (pun intended) a job at The Fish, WFSH in Chicago, the station offered me the job as his morning show co-host.

Years later, after my "slow fade," we interviewed Bart Millard, lead singer of MercyMe. Over the years, Johnny and I had seen Bart and his wife, Shannon, face some pretty big hurdles in life, including the death of her brother and their oldest son's struggle with diabetes. I asked Bart during the interview how he met his wife, and Bart said that they were friends for years before they got married. He said that he thought that actually helped them in their times of trial.

Bart went on to explain that one day he was explaining to one of his guy friends that he wanted to find a woman who was just like Shannon. At that moment, a light bulb turned on in his head: "If I want someone just like Shannon, then why not Shannon?" They started dating, got married and five kids later, still love each other and put each other first (after Jesus).

When Johnny heard Bart's story, he suddenly looked up across the broadcast counter at me with a shocked look on his face. I had no idea what was going on for him at the time, but he later recounted that he was thinking, "Why not Stacey?" It's funny because on our wedding video, Bart claims that he was responsible for us getting together. And maybe so, but we won't let him get too carried away with the credit!

Some of my friends who are having marital problems say they have the right to be happy, too, like I am with Johnny. I would never encourage them to divorce but rather to do **whatever** it takes to work to preserve and strengthen their marriages. It's truly not that one husband is better than another; what *is* true is that I am a better wife now than I was the first time.

My story is the perfect example of how God took the bad parts of what my human frailty and sin created and turned it into a tremendous gift for me and those around me.

When my 92-year-old step-grandmother passed away I heard Johnny call my step-grandfather to tell him we were praying for him. That is a great example of how Johnny loved me and my family. I reach out in similar ways to his family. Learning to fully support each other and each other's families is the ultimate good that came out of my past mistakes. My marriage now is not perfect, but we are there for each other, and we hold on tight to what God has given us.

Jesus was there for those around Him while He was on earth, and He is here for you now. Surrounding us with love, He shares the peace that He promised in John 16:33: *I have said these things to you, that in me you may have peace.* A relationship with Jesus is the ultimate in peace

Jesus was there for those around Him while He was on earth, and He is here for you now.

because He understands you right where you are. Jesus didn't say it was going to be an easy life. Ironically, Jesus went on to tell His disciples in the next verse: *In the world you will have tribulation. But take heart; I have overcome the world.* So take heart and know that you are loved. Take heart and be there for each other.

Taking my ailing Grandmother shopping probably should not count as a caring moment but it truly was because she insisted on using Sears brand laundry detergent and <u>only</u> Sears brand laundry detergent. She insisted on coming with me (rather than letting me just run out and get it for her) and even though I knew it would make the trip so much slower, I agreed. So we went to the mall, bought the biggest tub they had of the stuff and started out to the parking lot.

I don't know if it's still this way, but at that time and for as long as I can remember, the laundry detergent was located near the Parcel Pick Up entrance on the inside of the store, so that's the way we came out. I was holding onto my Grandmother's arm, guiding her with one hand and holding the laundry detergent with the other. We came out and were stopped by a man loading a dryer into a pickup truck, asking us for the time. I had to put down the detergent and look at my watch so there was a pause involved.

Heading on our way, I picked up the tub and just as we started to step off the curb, a large box truck came barreling down on top of us. The wind from the truck blew us back and we both stood there in shock as a man went screaming after the truck saying that it had popped out of gear. It smashed into a row of cars (not ours, thank God) but Grandmommie and I just looked at each other.

When I turned back to look at the man with the dryer in his truck, he was gone. If he had not asked for the time or I had not taken that moment, we both would have died. If I had been alone and not moving at my Grandmother's pace with much care, I would have died. Being there for her – with love and care – is what saved my life that day.

Someone once asked Jesus, "What is the greatest commandment of all?" A reasonable question, I would say. One I might have asked if I could ever get over being in awe of Him. Jesus replied in Matthew 22:37 - 39, *You shall love the Lord your God with all your heart and with all your soul and with all your mind. This is the great and first commandment. And a second is like it: You shall love your neighbor as yourself.*

This is where the simplest understanding of God comes in. I love God because He loved me first and He created me to love. I am often faced with people who are not only alone but don't believe in God. So I ask "Do you love someone? It can be someone who has passed on or a person you care about now but do you love?" If the answer is yes (and it usually is), then that person knows God because God created love.

You should know that there will be times that you won't know who is there for you but you will see or hear the results. When I was in my 20's, I was in a terrible softball accident. I won't go into the gory details but I was hit in the face with the ball and broke both sides of my upper jaw and one side of my lower jaw. Yeah, that girl could hit!

I ended up in the emergency room and I looked terrible. That's probably an understatement but the way my mother and father looked at me when they arrived, I would say it's probably right on. They took X-rays, stitched up my broken skin and finally realized that my palette was detached from the rest of my face so they called in the surgeon.

I was in the emergency room for a good six hours before they decided that I would have surgery to rebuild my face the next day. So I was rolled down the hall and put into a room. They didn't have any private rooms available and I must admit I really didn't care if it was private or not at that point. So they rolled me past my roommate and I saw what looked like a mummy lying in the bed next to me, moaning. Probably not the greatest thing I could have seen in my condition but she turned out to be just what I needed.

My mother was at my side the whole time, but after the

nurse came in and I had an IV and was getting settled, she needed to run out to get some things. I was told the medicine would make me sleep so I told her to go. I guess that was when the panic set in. Lying there, listening to my mummy neighbor moan in pain, thinking that I would never look the same again, I started some serious sobbing of my own. The kind that catches in the back of your throat but because of the damage was sounding out of the front of mine. "No, no, no, no, no." rang out of my mouth several times before I noticed that the moaning on the other side of the room had stopped.

I don't know the mummy's name and I probably never will but she simply said, "It's all going to be okay. You're going to be alright." With those words, the panic and the fear left the room and I finally slipped off to sleep knowing that everything was going to be okay. You truly never know where that care is going to come from or from whom.

Ephesians 5:2 explains that we should live a life filled with love for others, following the example of Christ who loved us and gave himself as a sacrifice to take away our sins. To lay down your life for your friends takes on many forms in today's world. It may mean laying down your work life (or vacation days) to care for a sick person, dropping off groceries at the home of a friend when you are missing groceries of your own or risking your feelings to tell them about Christ.

This could be the end of this chapter were it not for the skunk story I mentioned earlier. One morning, Bogey and I were walking around the back of the hotel (yes, the one I never want to live in again) before my early-morning shift. Since all of us were hired basically at the same time, they put all of their new employees up at the same place. Johnny and his dog, Gabe came around the other side of the building. We were standing there chatting when Gabe took off running.

Next, all I heard was a hissing noise, and suddenly, I couldn't catch my breath. Gabe had startled a skunk, and all four of us had taken a direct hit! We still had to go to work, of course, so I went upstairs and changed, tried to wipe the skunk oil off Bogey, and headed to the studio. To say that we smelled bad doesn't even begin to describe it!

Believe it or not, my mother and nieces were on their way that same day to visit me in Chicago for the first time. They still came but had to ride around in my car with the windows down and coffee grounds all over the car. (Hey, coffee grounds really do absorb the odor!) They took it in stride and we had a fun time. My point is – they were there for me. Still to this day, my nieces, cousins, and other family members know that when they need me, I'll come running and when I need them, the next plane is not that far away.

I hope that you know Jesus and know He is there for you.

What I learned the hard way is how to be there for someone when he or she needs me. I hope that you know Jesus and know He is there for you. And I hope you can be there, too, to catch someone's luggage if it falls off the tram, ride in their car after they were sprayed by a skunk, stay with them when their heart is broken, and help them to find the peace that is available in Jesus Christ.

And walk in love, as Christ loved us and gave himself up for us, a fragrant offering and sacrifice to God.

EPHESIANS 5:2

5

NOT EVERYTHING IS
WORTH SNIFFING

(Pick Your Battles)

*T*have a baseball cap that says "Sleeps with Dogs." Johnny, on the other hand, absolutely never wanted dogs in our bed. Bogey never gave him a choice. From the day that I found her (or she found me), she slept on my left side with her head on the pillow. It was like it was the most natural thing for her, as though she had been there all her life. Then Johnny came along and declared things were going to change! I think he forgot to make sure Bogey got the memo.

After we started to date, I had to go out of town and he offered to take care of Bogey overnight. He reminded me, "She is never sleeping in my bed!" I understand that lasted until she stood at the side of his bed and whined for three hours straight, and he finally picked her up. Not wanting to seem like Bogey had won, he then stated, "She can sleep in the bed, but only on top of the covers!" That was his compromise—until the time I got sick and he had to take her to stay with him. She did start out on top of the covers, but ended up an inch from his face, staring at him in the middle of the night. So he gave her a special blanket to lie under. Not good enough. The next time she stayed over, she slept under the covers on the empty side of his king size bed.

Then came marriage. We actually left her at the kennel the first night of our marriage so the topic of where Bogey sleeps would not come up and ruin our first night together. But that next night, there she was, sleeping on my left (with her head on the pillow), while Johnny was on my right. Marriage softened his will regarding dogs in the bed, and Johnny would be the first one to tell you that he loved it for the four-and-a-half years of our marriage that Bogey was with us.

Well, except for the snoring maybe. There were some nights when she snored more loudly than my husband but that might have to go into another chapter (about loving unconditionally!). So the compromise for Johnny went from "not in the bed" to "not under the covers" to "not on the pillow" to "not between us." We stayed with the last one until she was really sick, and she needed comfort from both of us (neither one of us minded at that moment).

Compromise really does come down to being content in any situation. The apostle Paul wrote, *I have learned in whatever situation I am to be content. I know how to be brought low, and I know how to abound. In any and every circumstance, I have learned the secret of facing plenty and hunger, abundance and need.* (Philippians 4:11-12). Paul's circumstances were totally different from mine, of course.

Compromise really does come down to being content in any situation.

He was beaten, imprisoned, and persecuted for spreading the Good News of Christ. His old friends turned away from him, and his new friends didn't completely trust him for a while. He knew what it meant to be on top of the world and at the bottom. But he knew how to compromise to the point of being content.

The type of compromise I am speaking about here is the positive compromise of picking your battles. David Dein, the past wisenheimer on our show at STAR 99.1 FM in NYC, says that his mother taught him to apply "TKN" to everything that he was going to say. Before you speak answer these three questions; "Is it Truthful?" "Is it Kind?" and "Is it Necessary?" That is the type of compromise that I am talking about here. Not the type of compromise where you change your morals or accept someone else's plan for your life (apart from God).

I am using Paul as an example because some people see him as hard-headed but the positive compromises in his life actually led to the writing of at least one of the gospels. In Acts 15:36-38, Paul and Barnabas were set to travel together and Barnabas wanted to take John, also called Mark, along with them. But, Paul felt that John had let them down by returning home early on a recent trip so he refused, holding onto his bitterness in that situation.

By Acts 15:39-41, we find Barnabas and John Mark traveling to Cyprus and Paul choosing to take Silas to Syria and Cilicia, effectively parting ways. Barnabas was willing to compromise and forgive John, also known as Mark, giving him a second chance. But here's the kicker; we find out later in Scripture that Paul eventually gave him a second chance, too. In the final epistle of 2 Timothy, we find Paul asking for Mark to come to him because only Luke was there at the time. He said to bring Mark because he is helpful in his ministry! That's a positive compromise turning out for the best for everyone!

We may not have the Gospel of Mark if Barnabas and Paul had not chosen to forgive what they saw as John Mark's failing them in the past and moved forward to lead more people to Jesus Christ. Is there someone you need to forgive or compromise with? We serve a God of second, third and fourth chances. Who can you give one to today? *Be kind to one another, tenderhearted, forgiving one another, as God in Christ forgave you* (Ephesians 4:32).

Sometimes compromising is as simple as keeping the peace.

Blessed are the peacemakers, for they shall be called sons of God, Jesus taught in his Sermon on the Mount (Matthew 5:9). But at times being a peacemaker is the least of our goals, right?

The first big fight Johnny and I had was over how to fold the towels. TOWELS. I could have compromised, learned his way, and kept the peace, but instead, we got into a knock-down, drag-out fight every time we washed towels. Not the greatest way to start a marriage *or* keep the peace.

So one day I was folding towels and as Johnny helped, I watched how he did it. That was our crossroad to peace because I decided to compromise. I would fold the big towels his way and the little towels mine. There was not another argument until the day I stacked the towels the wrong way. Then, instead of going round and round about how we were going to stack the towels, I simply said, "Okay," and turned them the way he liked.

Realizing I had married a person with "towel preferences" was one of the first steps to being a peacemaker through compromise in my own home. We have to prayerfully decide when it's important to compromise and ask the Lord how and when to do so. Johnny could see how important it was to me (and to Bogey) to have Bogey with me on the bed at night, and he was able to compromise and be at peace with his change of heart.

Towards the end of Bogey's life, the compromise about the bed worked the other way. Bogey started to disconnect from me, so I had to be content with having her close by in the bed instead of right next to me. Her first step away from me was that she wanted to sleep on top of the covers and would not stop fussing until I put her there. Then she wanted her own bed on top of our bed—probably because her old bones needed the padding. That was one of the most difficult steps for me. Still to this day I can't touch her spot in the bed without expecting to feel her warmth and love.

This act of disengagement on Bogey's part shook my faith because I was not supposed to feel this hopeless knowing that there is a heaven (and that the dogs we love are there). But it happens every time, and I'm not sure why: when my peace is gone, there goes my hope and my faith. This world is a pretty harsh place. We North Americans happen to live in a pretty good part of that world, but when all is said and done, something bad is going to happen in your life if it hasn't already, no matter who you are or where you live. It could be a phone call that drops you to your knees, the police at your front door, or simply your dog passing away. But it will happen, so what's the first step to fight the panic and fear?

While we still suffer with bad economies, terrible accidents, and separation through death, just take a few minutes and move into the presence of God. God is always with you. Overcome the world. Back to Paul for a moment and his advice: *Do not be anxious about anything, but in everything by prayer and supplication with thanksgiving let your requests be made known to God. And the peace of God, which surpasses all understanding, will guard your hearts and your minds in Christ Jesus* (Philippians 4:6-7). If you talk with God about everything, you will be moving into the presence of God and know that He is there no matter what.

If you talk with God about everything, you will be moving into the presence of God and know that He is there no matter what.

There is also the incredible knowledge that you will be able to help someone else in the future because of what you are going through right now. Every experience I have delighted in or suffered through has come back around so that I could help someone else through their suffering. Galatians 6:2 explains it all very well: *Bear one another's burdens, and so fulfill the law of Christ.* If you share the other person's troubles, you will understand that sometimes things happen in life and you don't understand at the time. But inevitably, someone who is already in your life, or someone who God will bring into your life in the future, will need what you have learned from this experience. Don't discount the pain or experience as useless because the person that needs your wisdom later will count it as priceless.

On that note, please don't ever forget that the world is watching how you react. We are never to be without hope because our hope lies in Jesus Christ. So, if you are acting like there is no hope or contentment or compromise, the world won't want anything to do with your Jesus. If everyone else around you is frantic and you are calm, others are going to want what you have. The apostle Paul says, *I can do all things through him who strengthens me* (Philippians 4:13). Don't doubt it!

I cannot lie and say that I did not ask why during the most difficult times, including the last days of Bogey's life. I believe it's okay to cry out to God and ask why. There is no greater pain than knowing that you will be separated from someone you love for the rest of your life on earth. If you are going through something that is painful and you don't understand, I know what that's like. We all do. If contentment and compromise are out of your reach, start with the pain and see where that leads you. Mine led me to writing this for you.

With all humility and gentleness, with patience,
bearing with one another in love,
eager to maintain the unity of the Spirit in the bond of peace.
EPHESIANS 4:2-3

6

STRAY VS. STAY

(Be Present in the Moment)

O nce Johnny and Bogey had compromised on the sleeping arrangements, Bogey slept by my side for the first five years of our marriage. On Saturdays, when we could sleep later, the three of us would lie there in what we called a "Stacey sandwich" – and that was one of my favorite parts of life back then.

Bogey had her way of getting the most out of every moment. She taught us how to stay right there. Some mornings, Johnny would roll over and stretch and moan, then I would do the same, then Bogey would emit this little moan that told us that she was right there with us. It brought great joy to my heart knowing that everyone I loved in that room felt the same way, and we felt it together.

Life can get away from you. I have spent entirely too much of my life worrying about things in the future that never happened, and fretting about things in the past I couldn't change. If you could track my brain waves, you would be able to see the moments when Bogey was present, when I was petting her, when she was my center of attention. You would've seen a calmness there in my brain that surpassed all understanding. In her unconditional love, she taught me that, no matter what I had done in the past or what was coming in the future, she was all that mattered in that moment.

She also taught us not to avoid the present because she had present needs. You never had to wonder what Bogey needed or wanted at any time. If she wanted to lie still, she would curl up in her little "curly-que," as Johnny called it. If she was hungry, she would let you know it was feeding time. And, if I was paying attention to someone else, namely my husband, when she thought I should be paying attention to her, she let me know. Another bed moment she created was when we had stayed in bed too long after the alarm. We were usually facing each other. She would stand up and put her head directly on mine so that it looked like I had two heads. That was her way calling me the Mayor of Lazytown and telling us we needed to get up!

We always joked that she was the queen of the house and ran everything her way. (And that was partially true!) But everything she did, she did out of love. When my tears would come (and over 17 years, they came quite a bit), she would always look me right in the face with complete empathy. She had no idea what I was crying about most of the time, but she knew something was wrong. Johnny decided to play dead one afternoon, and Bogey went up to his face to see what was wrong. She started licking his face diligently as if to say "please wake up!" Johnny couldn't help but laugh, and of course neither could I. I told the "play dead" story one day on the air, and one of the other people on the show joked that Bogey might have been trying to get the salt off of the dead thing before they carried it off. Maybe, but to look at her face brought comfort where there was pain and peace where there was none.

To see her face and feel her affection was the greatest example of Christ's love I have ever experienced on this earth. It was totally unconditional (as I will get into later) and 100% focused on me. Sitting in Jesus' presence must be much like that.

Bogey could sit for hours next to me, never moving, just being present. That's what I want for my life, and I pray that is what you have for yours. Just be present. Stay in the moment. We plan and plan and work and work, and what comes of it? We strive and miss everything that we should have been enjoying. They say that the next generation will be able to say that they enjoyed their families more and that material things were not as important. I guess that means they won't have my disease because I can't seem to stay in the moment when there is work to be done.

This is particularly true where I lived in the New York City area. The Northeast is brutal when it comes to taking time to enjoy life. I have been told that if you sit still there, you will be run over. While I loved living there, I needed my quiet time with God to survive. Staying in the moment is hard to achieve but so incredibly necessary, and I pray you find it in your day. I remember my mother reading her green *Living Bible* before bed and what comfort I found in that one expression of her faith. She knew the moments we were experiencing would someday be memories, and she still leads a life that reflects that belief.

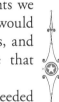

Staying in the moment is hard to achieve but so incredibly necessary, and I pray you find it in your day.

Jesus knew He needed time to be in the present and moments to reconnect with His Father. In several instances, He simply told the apostles to stay right where they were, and He went off to pray on His own. He was powerful enough to engage the Father right there in their midst, but He chose to live by example, showing us that we need private time in the present with God to live well on this earth.

One of the most well-known times Jesus left the disciples in order to go and pray alone was in Luke 22:39-46. Jesus returns several times to find them sleeping when He had told them to pray. Many theologians have suggested that it was then that Jesus knew His disciples were not strong enough to withstand the temptation to turn their backs on Him as He hung on the cross. This breaks my heart to think that Jesus was trying to prepare them for what was to come (as He is trying to prepare us) and these men were too weak (as we are) to prepare. In Luke 22:46 an exasperated Jesus says, *Why are you sleeping? Rise and pray that you may not enter into temptation.*

That's why the best way to start your day is in prayer and study of the Word of God. Your day is going to be full of temptation, just as mine is, so starting out by devoting the first fifteen minutes to God so that peace and praise will change the way you look at the next twenty-four hours.

Am I challenging you to take the busiest part of your day and slow it down? Yes, I am. Once the day gets going, it's easy to push what you believe to the side and ignore what you need for happiness. Showing your gratefulness to God first thing in the morning and staying in that moment (not planning the schedule for the day) will prepare you to take on the traffic, teachers, bosses, or anything else that may be stressing you out.

Staying in the moment is something that my family has taught me well. They know that I soak in the moments we get to spend together because they are so few and far between. I often tell my friends that I would love to come and sit on their couch, even if it is on the other side of the country, just to chat and drink tea. For me, that kind of moment is quite similar to sitting at Jesus' feet.

Oh, to have been at the Sermon on the Mount when Jesus sat and taught all day! Matthew 5, 6 and 7 contain the highlights of that sermon. Just the fact that the crowds stayed there with Jesus in that moment is amazing. In His longest teaching on record, Jesus starts out with what we call the Beatitudes. The first one in Matthew 5:3 says, *Blessed are the poor in spirit, for theirs is the kingdom of heaven.* Are you poor? If you don't consider yourself financially poor, are you poor in patience or in kind words? God knows what you need before you ask, but He loves for you to take the time to ask and to listen while He blesses you. Realize your need for Him today.

When we would go to the assisted living community to visit my grandmother, Bogey would jump up on wheelchairs, over walkers, whatever she had to do to enjoy the person on top of or behind the contraptions. The women would sit and pet her and smile, knowing that they were enjoying just that split second before she would jump up and run to the next patient. My grandmother enjoyed hours of Bogey's attention, and Bogey was there when she passed away, sitting in the chair next to me, staying in the moment.

I invested in Bogey's life because she taught me very early in her days that she would require these moments with me. When Bogey passed away, I was singing to her. The last sound she heard was my voice singing, staying present in that moment. Do I miss her now? Yes. The memories of her will stay with me for a very long time. I am grateful God gave me those moments and she taught me how to hold right there.

Whoever desires to love life and see good days,
let him keep his tongue from evil
and his lips from speaking deceit;
let him turn away from evil and do good;
let him seek peace and pursue it.

1 PETER 3:10-11

Johnny

Living outside of New York City can be one big adventure filled with incredible moments – if you embrace it that way. Stacey and I certainly did in more ways than one. From Broadway shows to Carnegie Hall to attending church at Caroline's comedy club, the city had more to offer than we could ever imagine. We even spent a Christmas Eve inside the brownstone where Irving Berlin wrote the song "White Christmas" (and Stacey does not remember his name correctly to this day). But the very first Christmas after we were married gave me a glimpse of what living life with Stacey would be like.

After church on a Sunday in December, we ventured over to look at the Christmas windows at Macy's Herald Square. As beautiful as they were the first time we gazed upon them, Stacey wanted to go inside to see what Santa's set up was like. I would call this Stacey's set up but I really don't think that she had planned for what came next.

As we were walking around the ornaments and Santa, Stacey spied a beautiful Christmas tree. In that moment, we both realized that we did not have a tree to set up. With her allergies, Stacey stays far away from real Christmas trees so we weighed the cost of the tree with our newly married budget and decided that this would be our very first tree! It was all very exciting to find the tree at such an iconic place and to share the memories that we would be creating below that very tree. That was until they handed us the box with the tree in it and we both looked at each other, laughing and shook our heads.

Once again, our record for big adventures was kept intact because we had taken the NJ Transit into the city and had to carry this huge box back with us on the train. Now that probably would have been less of a deal if it had been just one train but no, to get to our house you had to switch at Newark Penn. So we lugged the box to New York Penn, down the huge escalator to the lower level, onto the first train, down the stairs in Newark, up the escalator to the train platform, onto the last train, across the parking lot in Union to our front door with me shaking my head all the way.

Ten years later we still have that tree but more importantly we have the shared adventure of getting that tree home all those years ago. I thank God for my wife and her adventures every day and know that every time I see that tree, I will be reminded that you never quite know what is around the corner when it comes to Stacey — and to cherish every moment.

7

WAITING BY THE TREAT DOOR

(God Has a Plan)

Johnny and I have a small ritual that we do several times a day that truly helps us remain centered in Christ and the love we share with Him and each other. Johnny or I will simply say "three blessings" and "I'll start" or "You start" then we list off three things we are grateful to God for. What is amazing is how many times Mally is listed among those three things. You see, her story had a very, very unhappy start but God had a plan for her – and He does for you, too.

It was the day after Christmas in West Virginia and temperatures were below freezing with snow on the ground. Even though I will never understand why, someone took a tiny puppy with only one eye (that wasn't even old enough to be weaned from her mother) and dumped her on the side of a country road. When a driver noticed this tiny form wriggling around in the snow, they at first thought it was a forest animal in distress. Stopping the car, they scooped the puppy up into their hand and she fit perfectly in their palm. The warmth of the car was a welcome relief and the kindness of her rescuer was a gift from God.

While all of this was taking place, I was doing a news story on the radio about Petfinder.com. Researching the story, I fell in love with the website and would check it periodically to see who was getting adopted and who was not. I came across a picture of this tiny, one-eyed puppy named Chloe and could NOT stop looking at her picture. So, one morning on the radio, I surprised Johnny by announcing that I had found the dog I wanted to adopt to share our home with Bogey. His interest was piqued so he asked me about where I found her and what she looked like. That was when I dropped the bomb on him, "Well, she only has one eye." You could hear the silence across the airwaves and then Johnny declared "But, I don't want a one-eyed dog!" The other people on the show were stunned and let him know that they were stunned. So Johnny went on, "You can't play catch with a one-eyed dog!" and "It probably runs into walls all the time!"

The phone lines lit up and each person let Johnny have it saying "How dare you!" and "You have to adopt that precious little baby!" and that went on for a good couple of hours. Towards the end of the show, Johnny started to loosen a little on his stance and by the end of the show he had agreed to adopt this one-eyed love that I had found on the internet. After the show we had a meeting with all of our players at a local coffee shop so we loaded into Johnny's car and drove off, still talking about our impending adoption. David asked, "So, where is this dog?" I squeaked out from the backseat, "West Virginia." We all started laughing as David stated, "So, not only are you getting a one-eyed dog but you are going to have to drive 18 hours to get it!"

But God had a plan in that, too. The next day we went back on the radio, announced that we had been chosen as Chloe's new humans and she would be set to come home with us in two weeks. What we were trusting God for, we said – was someone to go and pick her up for us. The phone rang almost immediately and a voice on the other end of the line said that he loved road trips and would be happy to go get her for us. His name was Dave and he was currently unemployed so he had the time and was pleased to be part of the bigger God-story of this adoption.

When it was time for Chloe to be picked up, Dave came to the radio station to get the adoption fee and to meet us for the first time. We were blown away by his sense of humor and the overall peace he had about driving that far for a dog. Johnny and I also paid him a certain amount for gas and essentials. Well, it turns out that God had a plan in that, too! Dave was reaching a point where he was unable to pay his bills and the money that Johnny and I gave him covered the bills he was worried about. In other words, God blessed him for blessing us. Dave (who will forever be Uncle Dave to Mally) drove to West Virginia, picked up the pup, returned and we met him on the lawn of a Cracker Barrel so that Bogey could be introduced to her new little sister. Okay, Bogey was not impressed but we were immediately attached at the heart, one eye or not.

So what that person who dumped her on the side of road had planned as her demise, led to her coming into our home and brightening up our lives. We changed Chloe's name to Mally J. Belly because, if you have ever met her, you know that she flips right over onto her back to have you rub her belly (she will even do this for the vet!) And her first name and initial are a combination of my cousin's names Maggie, Emily and Jake. I knew that every time that I said her name it would make me smile because I would also remember their precious faces.

See, God didn't choose to bless me with children of my own but He surrounded me with children that I love. I know that when my younger brother Jimmy was born, I had a sense of what it felt like to love someone so much that you would give up your life for them but didn't know how to put that thought into sentences. But when Maggie was born, my 18-year-old mind totally understood that I would take a bullet for that kid. Then the twins, Emily and Jake, arrived and the feeling was suddenly times three. By the way, that feeling goes on for every niece, great niece and great nephew that I have.

I know that God feels the same way about each of us. In Psalm 139:16 King David proclaims that *Your eyes saw my unformed substance; in your book were written, every one of them, the days that were formed for me, when as yet there were none of them.* The God that I serve loves me so much that He knows every cell in my body, every hair on my head and takes the time to plan my days so that, when I am in His will, they are the greatest days to experience. I will never hesitate in telling you that He loves you in that way too.

So Mally settled in with Bogey and I caught her licking Bogey's head one night to clean her up and I knew they were going to be fine. Mally's rescue mom sent a note with her that explained her care, shots, etc. up until that point and at the bottom in big, bold letters she wrote, "DON'T EVER GIVE IN!" You see, Mally has a very strong sense of what she wants and when she wants it. Her pet sitters have reported back to me that she will stand for hours at the treat door, just waiting for them to grab a clue and get her a treat. Part of this may be our fault because I decided to call a friend of ours at the Star-Ledger, Joan Lowell-Smith, and she wrote an article about Mally and Uncle Dave that declared Mally to be Miss Personality Pooch of the Year. With that kind of press, you begin to believe you can have a treat anytime you please!

But I don't want to walk side by side with you and have you think that all of our days have been pure joy. As humans we have made mistakes that have taken us off path, believed the words of people who were not truthful and suffered great consequences at the hands of those we chose to love.

As a person who loves her God-given career in Christian radio as much as I do, I will tell you that not much rocked my world more than the day that Johnny and I both lost our jobs at STAR. The radio station that we had helped build had asked us to leave and the wringing of hands and gnashing of teeth could be heard around the world when I was quiet and alone with God asking him "Why?" The Hebrew word Azazel is a term the world would call "scapegoat" but it actually means "goat, go away." In that moment, Johnny and I were feeling quite goatish. It seemed as if almost everyone we had worked with had turned their backs on us, even though I knew in my heart of hearts it wasn't true. God brought each of those people into our lives for a season and that season had come to a close.

I'll spare you the ugly details, but soon after we were let go, the personal attacks began. Then the lies on the internet started. I learned a long time ago that you cannot change anyone else's mind about you (especially if they have the luxury of remaining anonymous) by debating them so our families and friends had to suffer the attacks as well. We kept our mouths shut only through the grace of God. And that may be the most important point of all, 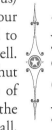 **. . . no matter what you are going through or will go through, God never leaves your side, period.**

no matter what you are going through or will go through, God never leaves your side, period. And He has a plan, even in the worst of times.

One day, Johnny and I both had a feeling we should make a video from our "kitchen table" that requested support for the radio station that had just let us go. It was a simple thing to do and there were still people that we loved working there because our feelings had not changed. But the most important thing about the video is that God still had a plan for that radio station and for the two of us. People in the tri-state area needed to hear about Jesus and that radio station needed to stick around so they could land there. After the video, we started receiving messages of support from across the county. People in radio, artists, people in our lives and those we did not even know started reaching out to us to say how impressed they were that we kept going and held no animosity.

Oh, how I wish that were true! Our human side **was** hurt and we had to put our boot on its neck so that it (the hurt) did not take over. There are a few people that know how hurt we were but they are good enough to not bring it out into the light. We are grateful that God brought us those individuals during that dark time. But wait, there's more!

As Johnny and I were asking God "why" we were still in New Jersey, "why" we were still unemployed and "why" there was no one there to support us – Super Storm Sandy decided to make its debut.

Now, we had lived through numerous hurricanes during our time in New Jersey but the weatherman was predicting it was possible that, hitting the coast just right, the storm surge could reach our home. I told my friends that it was like we were living an actual storm and a life storm all at the same time. Praise God that did not happen but just the possibility was nerve shattering. After the storm, it was not our nerves that we were worried about but those around us who were suffering. We saw people get together in churches and serve hot meals to those without power and those who were homeless because of the storm. Chain saws came out to remove trees from neighbor's roofs and radio people from across the country started calling us to get updates on what was happening.

God had a plan in the high winds. God had a plan in the shattered roof. God has a plan for every terrible thing that happens in your life so hold on with everything you've got. Now at Family Life Radio, we can look back and see His hand in everything at STAR. The reason that you are holding this book at this moment is because God had a plan for when and where it would be published. We are so grateful to God for sending His son to die on that cross so that we don't have to face life's storms alone. He has a plan.

For you formed my inward parts;
you knitted me together in my mother's womb.
I praise you, for I am fearfully and wonderfully made.
Wonderful are your works; my soul knows it very well.

PSALM 139:13-14

Johnny

In September of 2003, Stacey was still in Texas taking care of her grandmother and we had started dating long distance while I relocated to New Jersey to work for STAR.

When you go to a new place with a new workplace, there is a lot to take in and build while you are learning the ropes. I drove from Chicago to the Northeast at the end of August and arrived in NJ during the blackouts of that year. There was also an earthquake in New Jersey and the United States was at war with Iraq. To say that things looked a little bleak was an understatement but I knew that God had called me to serve here and I wasn't going to let anything stop me.

That included the difficult task of finding someplace to live. A few weeks before, I had researched areas to live and landed on a few as I began driving around to various addresses. At the same time, Stacey was in Texas on the Internet (the old modem, plugged into the phone line "Internet") and she was searching for a place for me. I literally had the newspaper laid out on the seat next to me while she pulled up directions and steered me to places that I would never want to live.

Finally, I pulled over to the side of the road to get my bearings and check my map. That was when Stacey asked me if I had heard of a town called Bedminster? "Yes, I think that is where I am right now," I replied. "Well, here is one at 11 Wendover Ct, Bedminster, NJ that looks really nice," she explained. Looking up, I started to laugh and realized just how much God had to do with my moving to New Jersey. My car was sitting directly in front of 11 Wendover Ct.

Further confirmation that God had a plan and was going to do amazing things as we obeyed Him.

8

Man's Best Friend

(The Art of Being a Good Friend)

ogey was the consummate nurse. When someone in our household was sick, she would lie perfectly still next to the person. If they moaned, she was right there in their face to make sure they were okay. Bogey and I had foot surgery the same week in 2007, and you can imagine the picture of her holding my foot with her little wrapped-up paws and looking at me with concern. Of course, I was looking back with the same concern, so the feeling was mutual.

I have some really great friends who could count as nurses, and I hope you do, too. No matter where I have lived in this country or if I have even had a place to live, my girlfriends have always been there for me. They stretch from San Francisco to New York and New Jersey, from Kansas City to Atlanta, from Pennsylvania and back home to Texas.

The day after Bogey died, I had to return to work because of a big event we had that weekend. One friend drove three hours and showed up at work to help me through my grief; she spent three days with me. When my grandmother died, another girlfriend flew in from San Francisco to join the many others by my side. If I start naming names, I am going to leave someone out here because I have been so incredibly blessed. Just know that I carry in my heart every time my friends have helped me, and that's what matters, not the words on this page.

My husband is my very best friend, and his stories of friendship could fill another book. Each year in the fall, he would surprise me with four pumpkins. He picked them out to represent each member of our little family; the biggest for him, next size down me, then Mally, and the smallest was Bogey. The year following Bogey's death, I dreaded the pumpkins.

One Sunday I attended a Fellowship of Christian Athletes ladies' luncheon and was driving home when I spotted Johnny outside walking Mally, our "one eyed-wonder dog." I rolled down my window and whistled at him. He suggested that I get out of the car and walk Mally home to get some fresh air. Strange request since I had on high heels but okay; I jumped out, took her leash, and he drove the car home.

As we were coming up the outside steps to our townhouse, I glimpsed the top of a pumpkin on the porch. I felt like a weight had hit me in the chest and the wind was knocked out of me. I gasped, "Oh, Mally! I'm not ready for the pumpkins this year." We stood there for a few minutes so I could get myself under control, and then we started back up the steps. I saw the biggest pumpkin first, so proud and tall. Then my pumpkin was standing there by its side right where I belong. Mally's pumpkin was next and had a big long stem that perfectly represented her snout.

What I saw next caused tears to roll down my face and nearly brought me to my knees. Among those bright orange jewels stood a white pearl of a pumpkin. Johnny had bought a white pumpkin to represent Bogey, later explaining that she is now an angel watching over all of us but still a huge part of this family. I am crying just writing this because my best friend knows my pain and takes action to make it better even before I know I am going to be in pain.

Jesus is exactly that kind of friend. He knows what pain

we are going to be in and does everything He can to stop it from happening or help us through it. That doesn't mean that we always follow along. We humans have a way of causing each other pain or causing ourselves pain that is beyond all understanding for our feeble minds.

> **He knows what pain we are going to be in and does everything He can to stop it from happening or help us through it.**

Really, if you think about it, Jesus was a pretty cool friend to those around Him when He walked the earth, and a very good judge of character. He often sat down on a hillside and taught His friends everything they needed to know to survive after He was crucified. Jesus didn't stand above them, looking down, and preach at them. He was on their level and even loved them when they did terrible things. In Matthew 26, Peter's denial of Jesus must have been one of Jesus' greatest pains. It was certainly one test of Jesus' friendships here on earth. At the end, when Jesus looked at Peter, His eyes must have shown all of the pain of betrayal from a friend. But when Jesus arose from the dead, Peter was one of the first Jesus showed Himself to.

Sometimes we have misunderstandings with our friends, and it becomes harder and harder to love. Consider the life of Judas and why, to this day, we still call someone who betrays us a "Judas." What you may not know is that theologians say that Judas was one of Jesus' best friends, and Jesus knew all along that Judas was the one who Satan had prompted to turn Him in. Even when Jesus washed the feet of His disciples', He washed Judas' feet along with the rest, even though *he knew who was to betray him; that was why he said, "Not all of you are clean."* (John 13:11)

Maybe your friends have said something that hurt your feelings and you have never been able to get past that. I have a big mouth, and I have said more hurtful things (not on purpose) than I care to count. My girlfriends are strong enough to point out what an idiot I can be, and we move on. But what if they didn't? A misunderstanding or hurtful language can lead to a lifetime of estrangement. Remember, God has the rain fall on the just and the unjust and we have to stand apart from the world in our friendships by forgiving each other.

Bogey and I had a misunderstanding from the first moment I picked her up. She yawned all the time. I often tried to get her to rest more because she was constantly yawning. People would comment when they saw her about how many times she yawned while we were standing there. And it was never just a little peep of a yawn; it was always mouth wide open, eyes shut, enjoying every moment kind of yawn. After ten years of living with the yawning dog, I finally decided to ask the vet about it. "Is she getting enough oxygen? Does she have enough rest? She yawns all the time!" I asked. She looked at me, smiled, and explained that dogs don't yawn because they are tired or don't have enough oxygen. Dogs yawn because they are content. Bogey was the most content dog on the planet!

But do you see where I could have mistaken that yawn for something else? When your friend says something that you take one way and she means it another way, discuss it and get to the bottom of what was meant. Don't let it run around in your brain for weeks and then finally confront your friend with your built-up anger. Life doesn't work well that way!

I do have a confession to make here that is not an easy one. People have tried to talk me out of it, and some have even condemned me for it, but I feel like I need to get it off of my chest. Some of my friends have even come along with me on this obsession, and for that I am grateful. Oh my, I can't do it! Okay, here goes: I absolutely love *The Twilight Saga!* Those books changed the way I saw writing and characters. The stories contained in each of the four books mesmerized me, and I even snuck out of bed in the middle of the night to read more. I am thinking of starting a self-help group for women my age who love those books by Stephenie Meyer.

One character is my favorite because she is the ultimate

friend: Alice. I have often said that I want Alice to be one of my friends because she has the qualities you should look for in a friend. She is loyal, makes you feel special, and she is there in the tough times. Alice is loyal to Bella before Bella knows she needs Alice's loyalty. That is the type of friend everyone needs! Alice also does everything within her power to make those around her feel special. The twinkle lights in the trees for Bella's disastrous eighteenth birthday are the perfect example. She lines the driveway (a long, long driveway) with twinkle lights. I won't even ask when was the last time someone lined a driveway with twinkle lights for you. But I will ask what those twinkle lights represent in the friendships you have now.

I have several friends who would qualify as a twinkle-light kind of friend. There are new friends who always know when I need a hug or a card, and even though they may live in a different state, they are totally in tune with my life. Some of my friends are the twinkle- light, fun and inspiring kind of friend, but I know if I called, any time of night, they would suddenly be the serious friend who would help me through anything. And then there are my friends who have been around forever and put up with some pretty disastrous things I have done but remain those twinkle-light friends through it all. Three very different kinds of friends, but friends I cherish in their uniqueness. They all make me feel very special. I am blessed to be their friend, and I try to make sure they feel blessed to be mine.

David and Jonathan are perhaps one of the strongest examples of friends in the Bible, friends that were willing to risk their lives to protect each another. Each time King Saul went against David, or even just threatened him, Jonathan warned David. Jonathan even challenged his father, wondering, "What has David ever done to you?" The king had no response. First Samuel 19:4 says,

Jonathan brought up David with his father, speaking well of him. *And Jonathan spoke well of David to Saul his father and said to him, "Let not the king sin against his servant David, because he has not sinned against you, and because his deeds have brought good to you."*

Now that's the kind of friend I pray that you have or will find.

It's great to have such a friend, but how can you also *be* a great friend to those around you? Maybe the Golden Rule applies. Matthew 7:12 says *So whatever you wish that others would do to you, do also to them, for this is the Law and the Prophets.* Being a really great friend means you will focus on the positive. Ephesians 4:29 says *Let no corrupting talk come out of your mouths, but only such as is good for building up, as fits the occasion, that it may give grace to those who hear.* No one wants to be around someone who is negative all the time. Slowly but surely people will start to pull away from that negative person. Something positive can be gained from each situation if you make the decision to focus on what is good. Paul wrote in Romans 1:12 that he wanted to encourage others, but he also wanted to be encouraged by others so that they could be a blessing to each other. That's how it works!

My grandfather died very suddenly. My mother called me and told me to get to her parents' house—now! I knew something was terribly wrong by the tone of her voice and the fact that she said "my parents' house" because she always referred to that home as Grandmommie and Granddaddie's house. I sped there in three minutes, and it was hysteria.

My grandmother had been in the shower for mere moments when my mother arrived and couldn't get an answer at the door. Grandmommie came out in a towel, soaking wet, complaining that my grandfather was asleep in the chair. My mother knew immediately that he was not asleep and called 911. When I got there, my grandmother had moved him to the floor. My mother simply pointed at him and said, "Do CPR! Follow my instructions." She was on the phone with the 911 operator, so I kicked into gear because I already knew CPR. But I couldn't get his jaw open, and there was something blocking his airway. Anyone in the medical field or trained in CPR reading this book already knows what I am going to say: he had been gone for a while. The paramedics arrived and loaded him into the ambulance, and I remember saying to God, "Your will be done, but don't do this to us!" My brother and I followed the ambulance to the hospital.

While in the truck with my brother, the first person I called was my friend Jane. I squeaked out the words "my grandfather" and the name of the hospital. She simply asked, "Do you need me to come?" Jane showed up at the hospital emergency room just after the doctors had told us he was dead, and she never left my side. Every time I looked up over the time from then to the funeral, she or my friend Susan were there cleaning dishes, making sure I was eating and sleeping, and taking care of my family. To say they carried our burden would be an understatement.

Dear Lord, please make me the type of friend that, when times of crisis or times of joy come, I am there. As you are for us, let me be the one who carries the burden of those I love and the friends that you have given. In Jesus name, Amen.

Greater love has no one than this,
that someone lays down his life for his friends.

JOHN 15:13

9

Sit!

(We Don't Walk Alone)

I love the movie *Lars and the Real Girl*. At one point in the movie, his "real girl" is "dying," and the neighbors all come over to visit. Once dinner is served, the women from the community sit in the living-room chairs and begin to read or knit. Lars asks one of them what they are doing, and they reply, "We are sitting. This is just what we do. We sit."

I am just like those women. I'm a sitter. Even before the year I spent caring for my grandmother; I would go into a house of illness or grief and simply sit off to the side until someone needed something. Being a Southern Baptist who was raised in Texas, anytime I hear of someone losing a loved one, I automatically kick into "what food do they need" and "where can I go sit quietly with them" mode. I am usually the one in a household who is grieving while carrying around a yellow pad, trying to make sure that everything is taken care of. Johnny knows when I get a heads up about someone suffering a loss because he hears my blender going from his office in our home. Normally he will just stick his head around the door and ask,

"What's going on?" He knows that my tears will be dropping onto my recipe card faster than I can wipe them away.

Bogey was a sitter, too. That was how we first bonded: just sitting together in a big, cozy chair. After Bogey passed away, my girlfriend Kari wanted to go shopping and I agreed. At one point I sat at Starbucks in the mall, alone, while Kari went to search for the last item on her list. I started listening to the conversations around me. *"I have to have that pair of shoes!" "She just doesn't look good in pink!" "My credit cards are maxed out, but I just had to have it!"* I wanted to stand up and scream that none of it mattered. I had lost the dog I loved, and people are talking about shopping? But I didn't. I slumped down even further into my booth and started praying for the strength to wait until Kari came back before I snapped. God is a sitter, too, and He sat with me. God knows exactly what we are thinking and how much we all need Him.

I would take Bogey to the nearby assisted living residence and the rehab facility to visit. She never hesitated to jump up on a lap in a wheelchair to greet someone, or to walk between the legs of a walker just to say "hi." I want to live in that way of thinking – never let anything stand in the way of making someone's day.

My grandmother had two ugly green velour chairs that I recall fondly. I guess beauty truly is in the eye of the beholder because she loved those chairs. There was just enough room in those recliners for one human being and one little dog. I can't tell you how many hours my grandmother and Bogey and I spent in those chairs, watching Johnny Carson or Lawrence Welk and enjoying one another's company.

I collapsed into one of those chairs when I realized that my first marriage was over. Grandmommie was sitting in one of them when I told her I was moving to Chicago. My grandfather died in one of those chairs. And Bogey and I were sitting in one of those special chairs when my grandmother took her last breath.

It had been a long road that ended very quickly when my

grandmother passed away. Months and months of laundry and medications and hospital visits led to hospice and morphine that the family had to administer. Her pain was excruciating and hard to watch, but the hardest part was yet to come. After all of that sitting, a single compassionate action would take my breath away.

Flashes of memory are all that remain with me today—and include morphine, nurses, and one late night when my grandmother was just cognizant enough to understand what was happening.

Everyone had been in to say their good-byes and to cry their own tears until my aunt, my mother, Bogey, and I were the only ones left. I took middle-of-the-night duty and at about 3:30 a.m., my grandmother woke up in pain and I put the drops of morphine under her tongue. Not fully understanding what was happening, she looked up at me with tears in her eyes and asked, "Why are you doing this to me?" In that split second, my mind scurried for an answer that might bring her peace in the midst of her pain. The doctors gave no hope, nurses came and went like clockwork, and I found myself in the place so many others have been when I answered, "Because I love you."

She died a few days later. I took Bogey outside while they removed her body. Physically she was gone, but she has never left me. As I have reflected on how she lived and how she loved, I know that I have never walked alone through my loss. I firmly believe that God would never create a love so incredible as a grandmother's and then simply sever it. Love lives on, and stories like this next one prove to me that she and my grandfather live on in Christ, and I am never alone.

Several years earlier, it was a warm spring day in Fort Worth when I decided to leave work early and surprise my grandmother with a special gift. She was hosting her sewing group at her house the next day, so I ran by the nursery and picked up a flat of flowers to plant in her front flower beds. I then snuck over while she was out getting her hair done and started planting them in the flower boxes my grandfather had built before his death.

As I was rushing to plant the flowers, the lawn men arrived to clean up the yard. Yes, my grandmother thought of everything! The mowers rushed across the grass as the weed whackers edged the yard. I simply acknowledged them and went right back to my planting. As I was kneeling down, placing pansies in one of the boxes, I heard a clear male voice make a very peculiar statement. As if someone were standing directly behind me, I heard someone say, "I owe you one." I responded with, "I owe you about ten thousand!" The most shocking part is I knew in a flash no one was standing behind me, even though I jumped up and spun around to see if the gardeners were there. But it wasn't the gardener's voice that I heard; it was Granddaddie's. The man who had taken care of that lawn and his family for years was thanking me, as only he could, for planting those flowers. But more than that, he was expressing his gratitude to me for assisting my grandmother in her time of need.

I knelt back down and starting working again, but you could not have wiped the smile off my face if you had tried. That quick connection with my grandfather lasted only seconds but was enough for me to know that I never walk alone. Jesus created the love between a child and grandparent and loves me enough to allow it to continue, even after their deaths.

When Jesus was resurrected, He made sure that we knew He would always be with us. One of the most beloved names of Jesus is Immanuel, which means "God with us." If we believe in Jesus, we shouldn't miss the fact that He walks with us each day. Hebrews 13:8 states that *Jesus Christ is the same yesterday and today and forever.* The Psalms say in 145:18, *The Lord is near to all who call on him, to all who call on him in truth.* I want Jesus to direct my steps, and I believe that Jesus can do great things in our lives

> **If we believe in Jesus, we shouldn't miss the fact that He walks with us each day.**

today. He walks with us today just as He did in the days of the Bible.

When we would walk the dogs, Johnny and I would each have a dog. As Bogey's health declined, I would carry her as we walked. The first few walks after she was gone, Johnny kept looking at me to make sure I was going to make it. I would clutch my chest and try to remember what it felt like to carry her, then cry my way around the block. It has become easier over time, and I know that I never really walk alone. In "sitting," walking, and living, we are reminded that God created love, and God is love. God shows us with little dogs, special ugly chairs, and special visits from loved ones that He is always sitting with us, ready to rescue and keep us in His care.

Two are better than one,
because they have a good reward for their toil.
For if they fall, one will lift up his fellow.
But woe to him who is alone when he falls
and has not another to lift him up!

Eᴄᴄʟᴇsɪᴀsᴛᴇs 4:9-10

10

SHARE YOUR TOYS WITH OTHER DOGS

(Give Back)

*S*naggletooth doesn't come close to describing Bogey's expression. I think by the time we got finished with all of the dental work, she had about four teeth left. Unfortunately, one was the lower canine so she always looked a little like a perturbed Elvis.

At about 13, her health took a turn for the worse. She was sneezing out these disgusting wads and having trouble breathing through her nose so I took her to the vet. She referred us to a specialist because it looked like more of Bogey's teeth needed to come out. Well, I had been through this twice before so I wasn't real sure why the specialist was needed but I soon found out. It seemed that one of the past procedures to take out Bogey's teeth had left a hole between her mouth and sinus cavity that was now infected.

The specialist explained that he would have to surgically repair her snout, including rebuilding portions of her jawbone. It gets better – the total bill was going to be $2300 at the *lowest*.

That's when the tears started and I asked for a moment to call Johnny. I should probably note here that this was right before we got married and he was waiting for the news as soon as I heard.

So I picked up the phone, sobbed out the story and then got to the bottom line. He asked me to repeat it one more time. Then silence… all that could be heard was my sobbing and his thinking. Very quietly he said, "Go ahead and do it." Then it was my turn to ask him to repeat it. "Go ahead and get her teeth fixed." Relief rushed over me and I went back into the office to make the appointment.

Now, don't think for one second that we didn't talk about this on the radio. It turns out that Johnny had been saving for a big screen TV so I had to live through all of the calls about not doing the surgery, sending Bogey to the taxidermist, and putting her on the couch so she could watch TV with him. But most people thought my future husband was the hero in all of this… and they were right.

I could never have financed that surgery. My time off to take care of my Grandmother had set me back years in the earning department and I didn't even have a credit card to put it on. But Johnny knew what it meant to me and he was willing to give of what he had to save my little dog.

Giving to someone who has less than you will always be a better way to live. There are so many experts on this subject that I could quote but I want you to go out and experience it for yourself. Take an opportunity to go and serve someone who cannot do anything for you. Don't expect anything in return, not even a thank you, and find out how much better you will sleep at night.

Giving to someone who has less than you will always be a better way to live.

You can't want for more when you are faced with someone who has very little. It can be your wake-up call or your calling in life but do for others with no expectation of what they can do for you. Open your eyes to those around you who need what you have – then give.

If giving is a hard thing for you to do, now's the time to look at the reasons why and perhaps to do something about it. I'm not just talking about money but your time, actions and faith are also on the table. When you choose to give back, you are being the hands and feet of God here on earth. He will walk beside you as you are following His edict to care for the widows and orphans.

As I wrote previously, I took off a year from my busy career to take care of my ailing grandmother. It's not like God gave me much choice, but I made a lot of wrong choices up until I moved back to Texas and said I would do His will by doing her laundry. Standing on my soapbox, let me say that the caregivers of this world don't get enough applause or credit. Now let me step back down and tell you about one heart wrenching day of care in particular.

My grandmother Katheryn was in assisted living and was having difficulty so they suggested I take her to the emergency room because my mother was out of town. It was not our first rodeo so we were not surprised when they put her into a room in the ER and ignored us for 12 hours; we knew they were super busy. In that amount of time, my Grandmother started having hallucinations, tried to injure herself and me and thought that the world was coming to get her. I was physically holding her down to the bed when someone finally noticed that we were having problems.

About six hours later they put her into a hospital room and my aunt arrived from Arkansas to take over. It was about 12:30 a.m. and I was physically and mentally exhausted. I had just experienced one of the loneliest, worst days of my life and now I had to drive home.

I got into the car and started the engine. The radio came on and it was a song by Jeremy Camp called "I Still Believe." The words told me that I was not alone and that no matter what I was going through in life, God was always there. It sang straight into my soul. I still believe. You can, too. He gave the ultimate sacrifice to save you so why not accept Him now? It's a simple prayer that will change your life. I can't let you get away without giving you this shot at eternal life and love. Tell Jesus you believe He is your Savior and that He loves you and died to save you. He knows you have sinned and how but go ahead and admit that to Him, then ask Him to come into your life and allow you to give more.

Giving is our way of honoring everything that He gave to us. We want to help others because He helped us first. Nothing too confusing here, I promise. Just know that walking with Him each day means recognizing those around us that need Him and need help. That's where you're sharing your faith and giving your time comes in.

We want to help others because He helped us first.

Give back what was truly never yours in the first place. If you have a hard time believing that God has given you everything in your life, wait until you lose what matters to you now. I have, at various times in my life, been destitute. Hurricanes have come along and wiped out the food I needed to feed my family. Hail almost took the lives of people I love but it definitely took their vehicles. A tornado blew through my hometown and left me hunkered under a bridge, my car packed with my belongings because it decided to blow through while I was moving.

I have set up a garage sale and watched people take things I had spent my (notice the use of *my*) hard earned money on for pennies on the dollar. Give someone what you have and God will replenish your every need. Not every want (even though He sometimes gifts us that way too) but your every need. I don't want to tell you about Corrie Ten Boom and the book *The Hiding Place*, I want you to go read it for yourself. Corrie, like so many other families, gave what they had during Nazi times to save Jewish families from death or imprisonment. My prayer is that I am strong enough to give that amount when the time comes.

God was with me in my giving in that dog nose specialist's office, in that Emergency Room with my grandmother, in that hospital room when my aunt showed up, and in that car when the radio sang to my heart. He has given us everything we have – what is He asking you to give today?

If your enemy is hungry, give him bread to eat,
and if he is thirsty, give him water to drink.

Proverbs 25:21

Johnny

One of our traditions is the naming of our cars. There is an old family story about when Stacey was in high school and a drunk driver hit her Corolla that was parked out front of her family home. When the police picked up the DUI suspect, he said "But I hit a trash can." And when the police told Stacey's dad he laughed and said "He's not that far off." So let's just say that before we were married, Stacey did not have the cleanest cars, let alone names for her cars, as we do now.

The motorcycle is Bella, we have had a GMC named Sophia, the car we have now is Alice but the most important naming took place when Frankie came into our lives.

It was in Chicago and I didn't have any idea about what kind of car I wanted. The search was wide and long. I asked my friends what they thought, scoured the newspaper on the weekends (yes, I still read the Sunday paper) and went on my own from car lot to car lot. Our friend Denise suggested that I go see her husband at the Mercedes dealership because they had some really nice used cars that had been traded in. Knowing that being in the ministry was going to limit my level of car, I hesitated at first but then decided that, if nothing else, I would get to meet her husband since we thought so highly of Denise.

When I walked out onto the lot, I saw Frankie first thing. That was not his name at the time but he was the perfect definition of a land yacht. A 1990 Mercedes 560SEL, he was a little rough around the edges from living in Chicago his whole life but he was the perfect car for me. For the next 10 years, Frankie was my car. Named after Frank Sinatra, he had this way that he carried himself that reminded me of Frank. Full of honor and pride, Frankie took me from Chicago to New Jersey which seemed pretty "circle of life" when you think of his name. I knew that I would marry and spend the rest of my life with Stacey when I was calm after she spilled a full cherry Slurpee into his front right floorboard. Now that's true love!

But all good things must come to an end and Frankie was no different. Each morning Stacey and I would stop by our local Starbucks and get coffee for our mornings. We struck up a friendship with several of our fellow travelers and our barista at that location. Having lived life alongside our friends at Starbucks, we knew that this barista was working at Starbucks to help his family have insurance after his job loss. Within the process of unemployment, they had also lost their home.

When we pulled up at Starbucks, the barista asked "why are you in two cars?" Johnny went on to explain that he was thinking about getting rid of Frankie and had to take it to the dealership today to see get him appraised. We no longer needed two cars because we lived on the NJ Transit line so, to save money on upkeep, Frankie needed a new home.

When the barista asked how much I wanted for Frankie, I told him that I didn't know yet because I hadn't had him appraised but probably a couple of thousand dollars — maybe! He said he might be interested and in that *moment God touched my heart and as we drove away in separate cars, I wondered how I was going to tell Stacey that I was giving our car away.*

When God tells you to do something He goes in front of you to pave the way. Stacey was totally on board so the next early morning, we told the barista that we would give him Frankie for $1.00 so that it was legal and above board. He was shocked and blessed and wondered why we would choose to do something like that for a person we met at a Starbucks. Without hesitation I was able to say, "Because God told me to."

Frankie died three weeks later. His engine froze up but the parts and metal were worth enough so that our favorite barista could put the money down on another used car. Frankie's legacy of giving lives on and, to this day, I know that we did exactly what we were supposed to do when we gave our Mercedes away.

11

IGNORE THE RED ROBOT
OF FEAR

(Do Not Be Afraid)

few years ago at Christmastime, large red robots were all the rage. They had three wheels and a remote control and stood about a foot tall. I saw one for just three payments of $29.99 on television, so I ordered one for Johnny. It came in a huge box, and from the moment it exited that box, Johnny used it to torment the dogs.

I can't imagine what they must have been thinking, because the robot talks, responds to commands, and has an alarm that can be set to begin any movement. Having been startled several times myself by the robot, I can testify that the alarm function is loud and obnoxious – and made me want to kick the robot right through the goal posts at the football field across the street from our house!

But to Bogey the robot was no big deal. Really. She would simply look at the thing like it was highly irritating; she wouldn't move when it was approaching or even bumping right into her! Johnny attempted several times to roll it directly over her, and she never flinched. Mally, on the other hand, ran for the hills when it came out and refused to be anywhere near the monster red robot, even if it was turned off. But Bogey really didn't care.

Same goes for the vacuum cleaner. Some people would tell you that it was my lack of vacuuming that led Bogey not to fear the machine. But she really was not afraid of anything as long as it did not physically hurt her. I could even vacuum the hair off of her and she would allow it.

Perhaps Bogey had nothing to fear because in the world we created for her, she felt safe. We controlled her environment, kept her warm and fed so she didn't worry about being inconvenienced with Johnny trying to scare her with a silly toy. Our human world, on the other hand, seems to surround us with things we are supposed to fear, even though there is no way these situations will ever come true. My Grandmother always said in her Texas accent that "95% of the things we worry about never come true and the other 5% you can't do anything about anyway."

Our minds build up fears that do not apply to our current situation, much like Mally and the big red robot that could not hurt her. Because it was loud and imposing, she built up a level of fear that still sends her under the bed when it is placed on the floor near her. Your red robot could be a fear of rejection, fear of loss, fear of failure, or just plain fear – but they all keep us from accomplishing what God has planned for our lives.

Did you know that it says "do not be afraid" or "you have nothing to fear" more than 365 times in the Bible? That's more than enough to remind ourselves daily that He has our best interest at heart and loves us more than we can ever know. The Bible also says that we are not to worry, but it seems we women (and some men) are making that an Olympic sport. "And now in the center ring, allow me to present the gold medal winner for worrying her little head off: Stacey Stone!" I can hear the crowd roar now. Listen to the conversation of the women around you and you will usually hear women's major worries: their children, jobs, spouses and money.

But in Matthew 6:27 Jesus reminds us *And which of you by being anxious can add a single hour to his span of life?* You can take that a step further and say "add a single hour" to your life **or** the lives of those you love. By worrying and being afraid, we are taking away hours from our lives and theirs. While we are on the subject of fear, I want to break down the healthy and unhealthy differences and levels of fear. The world can be a very harsh place at times, and I am not saying to smoke a pack a day, skip your mammogram, send your kids out to play without supervision or text and walk in Manhattan! That would be considered healthy fear. My mother certainly taught me not to walk up to a strange dog, not to put my hand on a hot stove and not to play with matches.

But the fear I began to create as an adult was an unhealthy type of fear. The kind of fear that catches you off guard and sends your thoughts away from Jesus and into the land of "I can't do this" and "what if?" A perfect example is being unemployed and not knowing where your next job is going to come from. Your mind builds up all of these scenarios that include what will happen if I take the wrong job, where is my next meal coming from and what if another job simply does not come along? Each of those is a direct slap in the face of my God who says He's got this. There is nothing to worry about because He created the world and created me to be what He planned for me to be. The right job, the next meal and the promise for your future are all coming along in God's timing which is always perfect. What I am

> **There is nothing to worry about because He created the world and created me to be what He planned for me to be.**

saying is that there is a plan of no worry and only healthy fear that you can hold onto with both hands.

What if there is something better for you than being a ball

of fear that is planned by God? What if the "big red robot of fear" that has kept you in your place for so many years was never meant to hurt you but instead meant to motivate you? Who do you trust to take care of your fear and make plans for your life?

I grew up in a time that is thankfully past where a woman went to college for her "MRS Degree" so a man could make all the plans for her life. But God never wanted us to rely on someone else to make plans but to rely only on Him. Jeremiah 29:11 says, *For I know the plans I have for you, declares the Lord, plans for wholeness and not for evil, to give you a future and a hope.* That is God's steady, reliable promise to us: Tenderhearted mercy, kindness, gentleness, patience and most of all, faith. When you have nothing left and the end-of-your-rope is coming near, faith can show you the way. Colossians 3:12 reminds us of that fact: *Put on then, as God's chosen ones, holy and beloved, compassion, kindness, humility, meekness, and patience.*

"But Stacey, it says nothing in there about faith!" Okay, but did you miss the holy, dearly loved, chosen part? Of course, I am speaking about faith in God, but that also means faith in the person that God created you to be. "Not me! I'm timid and afraid most of the time," or "God didn't create me for anything special, just this life I'm living now," rings through your head. Believe me, I've been there. I've actually had past employers send me such messages. "We are replacing you with someone who has more talent," was one of my favorites. "You don't deserve the life you have been given." "You can't get your Master's degree." "Why are you even here?" If I didn't believe that God doesn't create mistakes, I would have curled up in a fetal position on the floor after each of those were uttered (Okay, I did curl up for a little while to lick my wounds, but I didn't stay there and Bogey stayed with me while I recovered). The most important part was that it was not true. I had talents that God had given me and you do too!

At the Gospel Music Association awards a few years ago,

Chris Tomlin (the singer/songwriter with the most songs on the CCLI chart at this moment and more than 38.5 million downloads and counting) had just won several awards. He dedicated one to his college professor who told him that he could do anything that he wanted to do for a living, as long as it wasn't singing. I guess the joke is on the professor because God knew what Chris would do!

I want you to stop limiting yourself out of the fear that you can't accomplish something that God has set aside for you to achieve. I guess in some ways I am talking to myself because everywhere I turn right now, someone is telling me I can't write this book. But I know that God has set this task aside for me to encourage you and to prove to you that you can do whatever he has planned. And you can't let fear stop you.

That goes for the fear of what other people are thinking, too. This was one of the hardest lessons I ever had to learn and the biggest fear that I had to let go: that most people don't go around thinking about me or judging something that I am doing or wearing. Seriously, I walk into the closet each morning with the mindset that I will not put on something that I wore the week before. And yet no one in my office would probably notice unless I wore something for one week straight! I hate to admit this, but in the past I would wear an outfit one time for one special occasion like being on stage, and then give it away so that I wouldn't risk getting judged if I wore it again. Not only was it a major relief to realize that no one cared about the shoes I wore; it was also a relief that the mistakes I made and kept worrying about were long forgotten by those around me.

A perfect example involves an intense argument I had with my younger brother when we were still living at home. About fifteen years later, when my nieces (his daughters) asked me if we ever fought as siblings, I recounted this shouting match that ended with him slamming his bedroom door and having his collection of cherished (I thought) hot rod mirrors on the back of his door crash, crash, crash to the floor. Feeling terrible, I helped him pick up the mess. As I left I saw him in tears, still picking up pieces of some of his most cherished (I thought) possessions. When my nieces went home and asked my brother about this, he didn't even remember it ever happening! While it practically scarred me for life because I had done something to hurt someone I loved dearly, he couldn't even call it up in his memory. I had worried about it and let it drive me into a place of fear, while he wrote it off as something silly we did as kids. In other words, I turned it into a big, red robot in my life, while he put it behind him and forgot all about it.

In Matthew 6:25 Jesus says, *Therefore I tell you, do not be anxious about your life, what you will eat or what you will drink, nor about your body, what you will put on. Is not life more than food, and the body more than clothing?* There is nothing better than trusting in Jesus Christ and having a personal relationship with Him. I have a favorite quote that is not from the Bible which says: "Do one thing every day for Christ that scares you." That is the type of fear that you can celebrate, the kind that pushes past all of your walls and hesitations. What someone else thinks, what the world wants you to achieve, what the news keeps telling you to fear – nothing can keep you from living the ultimate life for Christ if you choose to live your life to the fullest. God has a plan for your life, and he never fails, so what are you waiting for?

To this very day, Mally will not walk by the red robot without watching very closely to see what it will do next. Some days, she simply sits and whines at it while it sits high on its perch in the living room. This world will surprise you and someone will try to tell you what God has planned for you is something you cannot achieve. I will slip back and start to worry about what others think or are saying about me. But the next time the red robot of fear comes around the corner, let's remember to tell it that we have the controls, and the controls belong to our God!

Even though I walk through the valley
of the shadow of death,
I will fear no evil, for you are with me;
your rod and your staff,
they comfort me.

PSALM 23:4

12

BEST IN SHOW?

(You Don't Have To Be Perfect)

ogey was not one of those dogs you would have ever seen at the Westminster Dog Show. She never had to be groomed, just bathed, and I will be forever grateful to my coworkers for putting up with her gassy-ness during a particularly pungent time. She certainly never would end up on any calendars after we had most of her teeth pulled and she developed a fatty tumor on her chest that we called her "lovely lady lump."

But to me, she was the most beautiful little dog. I knew her expressions and I knew what she was thinking by those expressions. Even people who have seen some of her pictures have been able to tell if she was happy to be there or if she was simply posing to make me happy.

While I have never expected perfection in my dogs, for most of my life in my own mind I thought that *I* needed to be perfect. I live in a family of supermodels. Well, not literally, but my mother is stunning, tall and thin. My aunt was Miss Fort Worth and is still gorgeous to this day. I got the gene of my forefathers that said that I would always struggle with my weight and have the average height very few find appealing. That's my description of myself but my husband would argue against that opinion all day long.

Where I say I am average, he says I am amazing. He calls me sweet and I say saccharine. "Exotic" would be one of his words to describe me and I just don't see it. My point is that anyone else besides me that looked at Bogey may have said she was cute with her bugged out eyes, but I thought she was **stunning**. I saw Bogey out of those deeper eyes of love that my husband sees me through. No one ever expected me to be perfect; that I took that on myself is my fault and I don't want you to take up that mantel!

I'll never forget a Christmas Eve when my aunt was wrapping a package on our coffee table. I had been taught by my amazing mother that each corner had to be perfect, every line of the wrapping paper matching and the tape preferably on the inside of the fold. And my mother's bows, to this day, are the best part of the decorations for Christmas. But to say that my aunt didn't ascribe to my mother's beliefs is an understatement.

I sat there with my mouth agape as she didn't trim the ends of the paper, simply twisted them up underneath and taped them to the package. There was no bow, the paper was wrinkled and nothing looked divine the way my mother's packages did. But, in that moment, I finally figured out that there was another way of doing it. Just like life, the perfection that my mother strived for and succeeded at, was not meant to be mine.

My perfection came from a totally different avenue and I had to find out what that looked like. In God's eyes, everything I do for Him is perfect. He knows how hard I work at what I feel him leading me towards and knows that I pour my heart and soul into it. Just like me looking at that little mutt and seeing love, I look at His words and see His love for me.

In Matthew 5, Jesus explains God's love through the Beatitudes. Don't worry because I am not going to throw major Christianese at you but I do want you to hear God's love through these words. My grief at Bogey's loss was overwhelming and God knew that. Jesus said in Matthew 5:4 *Blessed are those who mourn, for they shall be comforted.*

Even if you are not perfect, God is a source of mercy and comfort for those who have suffered loss. Maybe it was a job that you loved or a marriage you thought would never end. There are a lot of reasons to grieve in this world but you have to know that God is there, helping you through the pain.

It was a long time ago that I had to realize that God is God and I am not. Each day when Johnny and I drive out of the garage he asks me "Is it going to be a good day?" Over the years my answer has changed but the theme has always been the same.

"No, it's going to be a fabulous day because God is in control and we are not," was the answer I gave one morning as we were driving into a blizzard. That answer lets me know that God is going to do amazing things and I need to take the time to recognize them. He is in complete control. So any problems that come my way during the day because I am trying to be perfect, He is going to take care of. When I admit my need for Him, He is going to take over and make sure that everything works out for my good.

So what unusual requirements are you putting on yourself? Are their limitations that you have created that are holding you back from what God wants you to accomplish? Today I am asking you to give up your requirements and limitations and step out into an imperfect world to take a risk. Mess your hair up and see if anyone notices. Wear mismatched shoes and time how long it takes for anyone in your office to see what you've done. On the inside, stop expecting everything you do to come out perfect and stop beating yourself up about it.

> **Today I am asking you to give up your requirements and limitations and step out . . .**

One New Year's Eve, I was spending some time in Arkansas with my cousins playing charades. Something was wrong with my cousin Emily so I was trying to make eye contact so she would let me know what it was or lighten up. She simply looked at me and said "We are not always perfect like you think we are." Whoa! I never thought she was perfect but obviously I had made her feel that way. Whatever I said or did, I never wanted anyone else to feel that way so I turned down the rhetoric on my "perfect" life (that was anything but perfect) and started listening more to what was coming out of my mouth.

On that same trip, I noticed that Emily had a stripe of fingernail polish straight across all of her toes. It looked like she had taken a paint brush and painted her toes and her toenails at the same time. When I asked her about it, she laughed and said that she didn't like to focus on each toe so she painted them is one big swoosh and let the polish flake off her skin.

That is the best advice I can give you today for not being perfect. Paint your life all the way across in whatever you are trying to accomplish and let the non-God part flake away. It will fall off and what will be left behind will be beautiful because it is you.

The God who equipped me with strength
and made my way blameless.

PSALM 18:32

Johnny

I have a real issue with presents. Yes, the kind that I buy for Stacey and the kind that I buy for others. I get so excited about finding the perfect gift, that I'm like a little 5-year-old kid, "Hey, look what I got for you!" But for Stacey, presents are a really big deal so I try to keep them hidden or secret until the big day; be it birthday, anniversary or Christmas.

Early in our dating relationship, I dropped Stacey off at the airport to go home for Thanksgiving. Thanksgiving AND Stacey's birthday is in November. If you have had an opportunity to share our lives with us, you already know that Stacey considers her birthday the most fabulous month of the year (yes, that is not a typo, I said month). The countdown begins at the first and ends on the 24th unless she decides to stretch it out to the week.

Stacey explains that her love of her birthday comes from family birthdays when she was growing up. See, I married a woman who grew up on the same street or a couple of blocks away from her grandparents. So, every birthday and holiday was spent with numerous members of her family showering her with gifts. Yes, I blame my current predicament on her parents but I also know that the woman I love came from their love so I can't hold it against them. Now each holds special memories for us and Stacey hoards every birthday card she gets so that she can go back and remember the person who gave it to her and the year that was celebrated.

All that to say that, when I dropped Stacey off at the airport, the handle that she used to pull her suitcase broke off. It was pitiful to see her trying to tape it back together at the ticket counter so I made my decision about her birthday present right then. It would be a big surprise and I went straight to the store to purchase her a brand new set of luggage. Then I thought that, if she came over for dinner or to pick up Bogey after her trip, she might see it so I put it into the trunk of Frankie.

On the Sunday after Thanksgiving, I picked Stacey up at Newark Liberty International and she walked around to put her rag tag, broken piece of luggage in the car. Without realizing it, I let her accidentally walk back to the trunk as I popped it open. Needless to say the surprise was ruined but she was jumping up and down with joy so I couldn't be too upset. Just another way that I let the cat out of the bag when it comes to presents.

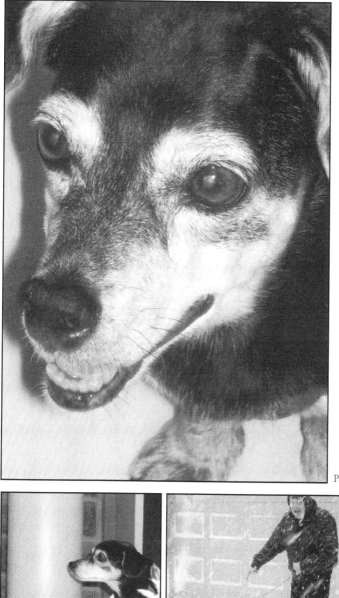

Precious Bogey

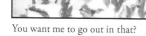

You want me to go out in that?

Okay…

Bogey and Stacey at STAR

Bogey telling Johnny who is in charge

Bogey asks "Do you have Grey Poupon?"

Bogey asleep with her sweater on that says Drama Queen

Bogey goes to
the museum
in Philadelphia

Driving Miss Bogey:
the day Johnny saved
by buying the stroller

Bogey at the shore

Young Mally says "So, I'm a little monster, what of it?"

Mally today is one happy, super loved, one-eyed wonder dog with Johnny, Stacey and Ringo!

With this precious face looking up at you, know that Genesis 50:20 is true for you!

13

THE ID TAG ON YOUR COLLAR

(Just Be Yourself)

Towards the end of her life, Bogey became the jumping dog. Her back legs were not as strong as her front legs, so she hopped, a lot like a rabbit does. It was very cute to see her bouncing along as our other dog Mally's behind, being part Corgi, always went side to side. Their "walking styles" were so different, and we adored them both. One thing to be learned from dogs is that they never change their personalities to conform to what we expect. Now, they understand the rules, but they maintain their same unique personalities and walking styles for their entire lives.

Who is asking you today to change who you are? It could be a spouse, a boy/girlfriend, a boss, a parent and so on. Have you thought about why they are asking? I'm not talking about detrimental things you do that are hurting you. If people want you to quit smoking because they love you and don't want to lose you, that is a good change. I'm talking about changing the things you like, the way you wear your hair, how to spend your weekend. These are all things you should be allowed to decide without too much interference. Now let's be reasonable here: your mother will probably never like your hairstyle if she has never liked it before. We can't expect miracles! But you can expect grace, and that is where being yourself comes in.

God created you. God doesn't make mistakes in how He creates us.

God created you. God doesn't make mistakes in how He creates us. God also wants you to be happy just the way you are, right now as you are reading this book. No "if only" you had a smaller nose or "if only" you had that other job or "if only" you were in a better relationship. Right now, God sees you as the masterpiece He created.

I really don't like working out. It makes me hungry and sweaty, and I have an aversion to those two things. But I do it, and I smile while I'm doing it, because my husband really loves to work out together and I really love him. So one Saturday, we were at the gym and I was in the stretching area with several other people. Two women who were obviously friends were working with a trainer. The trainer was pushing them to do more reps, try more weight, and go for longer. When she suddenly left the room to get more weights, you would have thought those two ladies' consciences had walked out as well. They started confessing to each other about how they had not been to the gym in a month, they were eating anything they could find to put into their mouths, and they didn't care what the trainer said, they were not doing that many reps! Then the trainer returned, and those two went right back to talking to her like they were ultra-workout queens! I literally had to hide my face because I was smiling so big! The way those two women acted around their trainer was far from the truth of who they were. They were "putting on airs," as my great-grandmother would say, and trying to impress the trainer (who of course they were paying to help them work out).

One reason my smile was so big was I had been there before. I'm not sure someone caught me and wrote about it in a book, but I have tried to impress a professor, teacher, friend, pastor and so on with how much I knew and how I was using that knowledge. But if you were to put my life up on a screen, you would immediately know differently.

God made me to be me. He made you to be you. There is no reason to hide from that, and there are several reasons to celebrate it! Ephesians 1:18 says *Having the eyes of your hearts enlightened, that you may know what is the hope to which he has called you, what are the riches of his glorious inheritance in the saints.*

All of your life's blessings will come from following the calling God has placed on your life.

While we can joke about hair and clothes and how we act in front of our trainers, this part is totally serious: All of your life's blessings will come from following the calling God has placed on your life.

Maybe you wanted to study education, but your parents wanted you to go into business. Maybe you felt pulled toward the ministry, but you just couldn't upset your boy/girlfriend by sharing your true feelings. Our culture will pull us in many different directions, but the greatest peace in life is being in God's will.

When I said "calling" in the previous paragraph, what did you think about? Your calling could be defined as the thing that is the center of your life. Money is not your calling. Psalm 62:10 says *Put no trust in extortion; set no vain hopes on robbery; if riches increase, set not your heart on them.* God couldn't be much plainer than that. You can't confuse your self-worth with your net-worth. What is in the bank has nothing to do with the person God made you to be. Being yourself and putting Christ's love at the center of who you are will change everything. In 2 Corinthians 5:14, the apostle Paul wrote, *For the love of Christ controls us, because we have concluded this: that one has died for all, therefore all have died.*

Everyone who knows me knows I love celebrating my birthday. I was born right before Thanksgiving, and I love to celebrate every year I am on this earth. It's all my parents' fault because each year we would have these big family birthdays. Every person would have their special party on their special day with relatives, cake, and presents. Those are some of my happiest memories with some of the most wonderful people God put into my life.

But there are some people in my life that think my birthday obsession is ridiculous, and that a woman my age should not be enjoying the occasion so much. But what's really cool is my focus on my birthday makes me enjoy the complainers' birthdays just as much! I love to create theme birthdays for those I work with, send special presents to my friends across the country, and generally have a great deal of fun with the day of their births. I am not going to change that part of myself because someone else thinks I am getting too old. That is part of who I am, and when I am seventy, it will still be part of who I am.

What part of yourself have you given up to be with someone else? What do you want back? When did you stand up for yourself and say no to the changes? First Peter 4:10 states *As each has received a gift, use it to serve one another, as good stewards of God's varied grace.* That verse points out that other people are actually being hurt by you not being yourself. If you won't hold on to what makes you special for you, do it for them. God is expecting you to bless others by passing on your gifts to them, so it's time to step up, say I am who I am, and live for love!

This is the day you decide what your contribution to this world will be.

When you look back on your life six months from now, I want this to be a defining moment for you. This is the day you decide what your contribution to this world will be. Philippians 1:27 explains

Only let your manner of life be worthy of the gospel of Christ. Look around you. What are you a credit to now? Through your character you will say lots of things, do lots of things, and choose not to accomplish some things, but what will your life look like when it is all said and done? Philippians 2:5 goes on to say: *Have this mind among yourselves, which is yours in Christ Jesus.* That actually makes it clearer because Jesus was all about the love.

A lot of people ask me about radio. They want to know what time I get up in the morning, how many hours I work during the day, and how I got into it in the first place. The highest compliment someone can give me is to say, "I feel like I already know you." Being real is a prerequisite of being successful in broadcasting, and it is the hardest thing to pull off. When that microphone goes on, something in our puny human brains tells us that we have to be "on" as well. That means changing your voice (or "puking," as we call it), making up a life you think others want to hear about, and sounding like you are all that. But years of research have shown people really want to hear people on the radio being themselves. That's where the tough part comes in because, if you are sharing who you are, that means warts and all.

So my years of radio have told me that people like me just the way that I am. God has an exquisite sense of humor when it comes to our lives; after all, he put this native Texan on a New York City radio station for a time. No one else would have wanted to take responsibility for that one but God! People ask how I got there, and the only answer I have is "God." *Trust in the Lord with all your heart, and do not lean on your own understanding. In all your ways acknowledge him, and he will make straight your paths.* That's from Proverbs 3:5-6 and says it all.

Being real translates into every part of my life. Sometimes someone will treat me like I'm a celebrity; I am so far from a celebrity it is not even funny! But there are times when someone will get excited to see me and say things like "you're so glamorous" or "you are beautiful," and I always smile and try to redirect the conversation to them and their lives. But one Sunday it did not work that way. It was Harvestfest at Madison Square Garden. Johnny and I were to visit backstage with MercyMe after the message, but what we didn't know was that security would meet us at the front gate and take us to the VIP section. A guy with an earpiece declared "I have them and we are moving!" After inquiring whether they truly knew who we were, they whisked us to our special seats, and several people around us were so excited that we were there. They went on and on about how wonderful it was to meet Johnny and I and how honored they were to sit near us.

After the message, we went to the side of the stage to wait for MercyMe's manager and, while we were waiting, a woman named Gloria came up to me and was shaking. She exclaiming how thrilled she was to meet me and I shook her hand for about three minutes as she went on and on about how glamorous I was and how she wished she could be this glamorous. On and on she went while I tried to get a word in edgewise, but after the manager appeared and took us backstage, I felt pretty good about myself. Let's just say that I was starting to believe everything that was being said about us. Visiting with the MercyMe guys, I had an extra wide smile on my face because I was so glamorous and they were honored to speak with us!

Fast forward about an hour and a half. Johnny and I return home and I put on my house dress. If you don't know what a house dress is, you are not from the southern part of the United States! It is a dress you would never wear outside of the house. For obvious reasons, it stays indoors and is usually very comfortable. When I went into the den to watch the news, the couch looked funny. It had little red dots all over it. Our Bogey had chewed a red treat all over my fake suede couch. Off I go into the kitchen, put on my dishwashing gloves, get out the cleaner, and grab a scrub brush. I'm cleaning the red treat off the couch and suddenly I just burst out laughing. Johnny comes upstairs to see why I have lost my mind (again) and while I am still scrubbing away in my house dress and yellow gloves, I tell him, "I'm so glamorous!" God has a way of leveling the playing field and keeping us humble when we can't do it for ourselves.

But I do not account my life of any value nor as precious to myself, if only I may finish my course and the ministry that I received from the Lord Jesus, to testify to the gospel of the grace of God (Acts 20:24). That is what I was called to accomplish. Having been on Christian radio makes it easier than other jobs to "tell others the Good News," but you can be a light for Christ no matter where you are in life.

Don't change who God made you to fit into society because society will change and you will be running behind, trying to change with it again and again. You are who you are for a reason. Ask Him today to tell you what that reason is.

Love one another with brotherly affection.
Outdo one another in showing honor.

ROMANS 12:10

14

BE WILLING TO GIVE UP YOUR CRATE

(Serving Others Is the Greatest Gift)

When you love a creature who ages faster than you do, there can be some pretty rough nights.

One particular night, I thought was Bogey's last. She had a seizure right around midnight, and after that I couldn't get her comfortable. Johnny and I had a great debate the next day about whether she was experiencing stomach upset or stroke-like symptoms, but the story that unfolded is much larger than the health-related issues she was going through.

About 1:00 a.m., I took Bogey downstairs so that Johnny could sleep. Bogey laid quietly on my chest for about thirty minutes before her pain returned. I tried different positions, different temperatures in the room, different blankets just to find some comfort for her—and sleep to go along with it. Nothing stopped her little body from convulsing each time the pain started in.

About 3:00 a.m., I was in tears and just needed to be in the same room with the rest of our family; so I carried her upstairs to the bedroom where Johnny and Mally were sleeping. Instead of lying in the bed next to my husband and waking him up, I spread a blanket out on the floor and tried the "lying on my chest" trick again. It didn't work. So I tried the "lying on the floor next to me" position. She still was not happy.

Then I heard a little peep from inside Mally's crate. Mally came to us from the dog rescue fully crate-trained, so she slept in her nice little bed while Bogey, as you know, slept in the bed with us. Mally had never asked to get out of her crate, so I reassured her that her sister was okay and that she should go back to sleep.

For the next thirty minutes I sat straight up with cradling Bogey around the front of my neck, providing pressure on the area she seemed to be favoring. But she finally pushed herself off of me and went to see what Mally was still whimpering about. Not wanting two upset dogs, I opened the door to Mally's crate and laid down exhausted on the floor. Bogey walked slowly over to the open door and stared in. Mally kissed her on the head and moved out of the crate to lie next to me. Bogey stepped inside that enclosure for the first—and last— time in her life. She curled up in a little ball and went to sleep for three peaceful hours.

I had absolutely no idea what Bogey needed. I knew only she was in pain and that we had to wait for the vet to open before I could get her help. What I didn't know was that Mally knew exactly what Bogey needed and was willing to hand over her personal bed to Bogey in her moment of need. Any other day, Mally would have never relinquished her crate but, in love, she knew that both Bogey and I needed to be served in that moment.

Look around you. There are people who need something that you have; they need to be served; they need your crate. In Matthew 25:34-40, Jesus tells us that serving others is the way to serve him. *Then the King will say to those on his right, 'Come, you who are blessed by my Father, inherit the kingdom prepared for you from the foundation of the world. For I was hungry and*

you gave me food, I was thirsty and you gave me drink, I was a
stranger and you welcomed me, I was naked and you clothed me,
I was sick and you visited me, I was in prison and you came to me.'
Then the righteous will answer him, saying, 'Lord, when did we
see you hungry and feed you, or thirsty and give you drink? And
when did we see you a stranger and welcome you, or naked and
clothe you? And when did we see you sick or in prison and visit
you?' And the King will answer them, 'Truly, I say to you, as you
did it to one of the least of these my brothers, you did it to me.'

Each day, in each of our worlds, we can find an opportunity
to serve the least of these. Now don't start with the excuses.
You have the time, money or simple listening ear that someone
else needs. Believe me, Mally did not want to get up out of her
nice, warm nest to allow Bogey a place of comfort. She showed
complete love and service in that moment and, as her human,
I was humbled to be part of it.

Sometimes, when you are serving another, you will find
that *you* are actually the one being served. Right after I started
working in New Jersey, God opened a door for me to help
someone; so I decided
to take the risk and step
through it. My mother had
sent me an e-mail from
a member of our church
talking about his wife,
Melissa, and their love
for Jeremy Camp's music.

**Sometimes, when you
are serving another,
you will find that *you*
are actually the one
being served.**

Without going into too many private details, Melissa had
cancer, and they found the message in Jeremy's music to be
uplifting during this trying time. Jeremy Camp's first wife (also
named Melissa), had passed away from cancer, so they felt a
bond with him and his music. Well, come to find out that
the radio station I was working for was presenting a concert at
the Jersey shore with Jeremy Camp, so I asked my mom if she
thought that Kyle and Melissa would like to come.

In His special way, God has already planned for them

to travel for this event. When mom asked, Kyle said that his in-laws had given them two airline tickets to anywhere in the United States and would keep their little girls so they could come. Of course, they had no idea where they were going when they received the tickets, so my invitation through my mom made it clear to them how God wanted them to use those two plane tickets.

A few of my coworkers, friends, and I arranged for their hotel, gifts for their trip, tickets to the concert, and a private Meet-n-Greet with Jeremy. We thought we had done everything that God had wanted. So I picked them up at the airport and headed to the shore, but if you have ever driven in Jersey, you know where this is going. I accidentally got on the Garden State Parkway going in the wrong direction and ended up having to call my wonderful husband to figure out how to get turned around and headed south.

After a while, Melissa needed a restroom, so I pulled over at a rest stop and we went in. There was a line for the ladies' room (surprise, surprise!), so we chatted about life while we waited. Our conversation led to the snacks that were lined up along the shelves where we were standing. I asked her if looking at them made her feel worse because of the chemo.

Melissa looked me in the eyes and said, "Actually, my medication has been really well balanced, so I haven't had any problems this time. We have been really blessed." She went on to say that the other patients around her during chemo were really suffering, but I must admit that I didn't hear most of the rest of the conversation because the air had just been sucked out of my lungs. Here was my friend who was facing the possibility of losing her life and leaving behind her husband and two small children, and she could say that she was really blessed by something.

I was ashamed, amazed, and embarrassed all at the same time—and my perspective on life was changed forever. Anything that I had to complain about flew out the window—and still does when I think about everything that Melissa said in that one statement. Here I was, thinking that I was doing everything for them but, in truth, God just did something for me too, by opening my eyes and changing my point of view forever.

I was ashamed, amazed, and embarrassed all at the same time—and my perspective on life was changed forever.

Melissa passed away on February 12, 2005, just seven months after their trip to meet Jeremy Camp. I would love to tell you that, since Melissa's comment that day, whenever God prods me to help someone, I always rise to the task. But that is not true. I have prayed for a long time for God to give me the wisdom or holy awareness to connect with others' hearts like He does, so that I can know how best to serve them. But, as the next moment proves, I still grumble and push back when He gives me His eyes.

In New Jersey drivers are not allowed to (or you might say they don't *have* to) pump their own gas. One afternoon on the way home from the shore, I stopped on the parkway to get gas (different trip to the shore, different rest stop, same parkway). The gas station attendant approached my car window, and I told him, "Twenty dollars of regular, please." I had been listening to the new Chris Tomlin CD *Hello Love!* and letting these wonderful songs about God and love fill my car. Then this overwhelming feeling hit me: *Give him the CD!* I would love to tell you that I took it out, put it into the case, and handed it over, but instead I thought, "No, I just got this CD and want to listen to it! Besides, he might laugh." The fear of someone laughing stopped me when God wanted me to partner with him in a miracle.

Then the attendant walked up to my window and said, "I really like that music." He walked away as I shook my head. Again I heard, *Give him that CD!* At that moment I can't say I had much choice, so I took the CD out of the player, put it in the case, and waited. One more time the thought came, *Hand him that CD!* So when he came back for payment, I handed him the twenty dollars and then handed him the CD, mumbling something about how he should enjoy it.

What other people think and the fear of rejection sometimes stops me from obeying God. But Bruce Wilkinson writes in *You Were Born for This,* that the fear I speak about is actually a cue to move ahead because God is doing something great. (If you haven't read his book, read it right after you finish this one! It will change your life!) I never saw that gas station attendant again, so I can only hope and pray that God touched his heart and life through Chris Tomlin's music. But after that incident, I started recognizing the miracles God wanted me to partner in with Him. I started to open up to those nudges from the Lord in a way I never had before.

My heart broke one morning for one of my coworkers as he and I were having a conversation about his wife. She had injured herself, and I asked how she was doing after her doctor visit the day before. He expressed his relief in knowing it was not a permanent injury and that she was going to heal. Then his tone turned to defeat as he expressed the strongest wish on his heart: that his wife no longer had to work at her current job. They had children at home and he wished she could stay home with them. But most of all, her job was hurting her health, and it scared him that she had to work in order to keep their family afloat financially because he was in full-time ministry.

I told him I understood, even though I really didn't, and soon returned to my desk. Sitting in my chair, I had this overwhelming feeling of connection and empathy for him and his family. I bowed my head and simply said, "Lord, I have enough, but give me what he needs for his family so I can help them." Then I was reminded of another family, and I prayed, "Lord, I have enough. You have given me all I need. Please give me what he needs so I can help this family. I have enough, so I also want to help this other coworker who I know has not had a raise in three years. Please give me the means to do that."

By the time I made my own sacrificial list, I had basically

given away all my salary, but that was not what God was calling me to do. God wanted me to work harder and spread his Word farther, and he would help me take care of these three families. That statement, "I have enough" stayed with me for the rest of my radio program and brought me a peace that I had been missing for a while.

After the four hours of radio programming for which I am responsible was done, I went back to my desk to a stack of mail from the day before. It was the same old credit card offers, training invitations, and packages from publicists that I see daily. But I always give each one attention, even if it is shredding, because someone in another job put a lot of effort into the information contained and the mailing provided.

The last package I opened was from a friend of mine who is a great publicist and always knows what type of books and authors our radio station specializes in. I had saved this one for last. Little did the publicist or I know God was partnering in this miracle envelope that day. I opened the package, read the title of the book, and sat back in my chair astonished.

The book that emerged from the wrapping was written by Bob Perks and was entitled, *I Wish You Enough.* I wish you enough! It felt like a direct message from God saying my prayer had been answered, that He was going to provide not only enough for me but also enough for these other three families. God doesn't need me, but He does want me, and I am going to do everything within my life

It felt like a direct message from God saying my prayer had been answered . . .

to watching for God's nudges to help others. God doesn't even need me to work harder; He just needs me to trust in Him and serve others. Each day I lay down my life (my "enough") to serve others.

I pray that God opens the doors and lays it on your heart to serve those around you and those in foreign lands. It will change your life forever.

> *This is my commandment,*
> *that you love one another as I have loved you.*
> *Greater love has no one than this,*
> *that someone lays down his life for his friends.*
>
> JOHN 15:12-13

15

ALWAYS AT YOUR SIDE

(Somebody Loves You)

his chapter may be the most important message of the entire book because I want you to realize that someone loves you. Whether they are living or deceased, dog or human, doesn't matter but the love they have for you does.

When you realize that you are going to lose someone, you start to pay attention to the little things. I started to memorize the wet footprints that Bogey would leave behind. I would studiously follow her and my husband as they sloshed their way through the yard onto the sidewalk to see how their steps would intertwine. It was like a piece of artwork to me and a perfect example of how our lives are all joined by love.

Maybe it's a smell that you've encountered with someone you love in the room or maybe a moment when you knew that the person holding you loved you no matter what. With dogs, it's sometimes a look that tells you that you are truly adored. While I was walking behind my love and Bogey, she would often look back at me, just making sure that I was still there. That look captured everything that was our relationship because she knew that I was there when she needed me and I wanted to be there.

When it was time for Bogey to lose her struggle to live, I carried her into the room and laid her in her favorite bed. I talked to her about heaven and what she had meant to me then I sang to her as she lost her life. Walking out to the car, I crumpled and my husband put his arm around me as I screamed out all of the pain of the whole experience. Pain I never thought I could endure and pain that seared a hole in my chest for months.

But the most shocking part of this loss was that I never felt the love leave. In the past, I have wondered with those that I have lost, if the level of love in my life would go down. When you are a baby or small child, it seems that the world is full of love just for you. Then you hit elementary school, middle school and high school and find out it's not your world of love that you have to live in. But love is still there, even as you lose your grandparents, parents or your friends to death. I have a favorite saying that comes from a song that we sang in choir and I remind myself of this a lot because I have a whole host of saints rooting for me. "Let those who've gone before us find us faithful." But most important, let those who were left behind feel loved.

The love never leaves and I can say with all honesty that there is someone who loves you right now. I loved you enough to sit down at this computer for hours on end and write this book. I prayed that you would pick it up and that these pages would fill your soul with whatever you are missing. If you are the only person that ever reads these words, then this book has served its purpose. My capacity to love you is my gift to you so I know that somebody loves you.

But the God of love is the ultimate example of that somebody who loves you. He created those original relationships so that you would know what love feels like. Even if your parents were not the greatest parents in the world, He is – so take a deep breath and know that Someone understands your pain at what you feel is a lack of love.

My friend Reverend Rob Cruver from Zarephath Christian Church told a story of a dream where he was sitting at the kitchen table with his wife Deb, his mom and dad. His parents had passed away years before and when he awoke, he felt a desperate need to go back to that place. He wanted to be "son" again and feel that love and kindness he felt in life at that time and in that dream.

God wants that for you. He wants you to know that you are His son or daughter and that the kindest, most loving place is with Him at His kitchen table. The answers to all of life's questions are there and everyone that you have ever loved who believed in Christ. When life is too hard to handle, it really is okay to sit for a while and put yourself in one of those chairs. If you need it to be a high chair to fully feel the love, go ahead. I'm not one to judge. But take the time to know that you are loved.

Jesus said it best in Matthew 7:9-11 *Or which one of you, if his son asks him for bread, will give him a stone? Or if he asks for a fish, will give him a serpent? If you then, who are evil, know how to give good gifts to your children, how much more will your Father who is in heaven give good things to those who ask him!* Do you accept today that God is your biggest fan and wants only what is good for you?

As you sit at God's kitchen table, how do you talk to him? You need to acquire the ability to pray for yourself and feel the love of an answered prayer. Psalm 138:3 says *On the day I called, you answered me; my strength of soul you increased.* So, when you feel like you are lacking in the love department, ask boldly for the love that you need. It's there; you may just need God to point it out to you.

When my Grandfather died, I remember the paramedics taped his hands together so they wouldn't fall off the gurney as they wheeled him to the ambulance outside their home. It bothered me that he couldn't move, then I bowed my head and simply prayed, "God, I don't know how I am going to survive this but let your will be done." From every time I had spoken or sung the Lord's Prayer, the words from Matthew 6:10 were what came back in one of my greatest moments of crisis, *Your kingdom come, your will be done, on earth as it is in heaven.*

I didn't like God's will in that moment but I knew that, as long as His will was done, I could survive. The "Why's" will have to wait for God's kitchen table and I am good with that.

The "Why's" will have to wait for God's kitchen table and I am good with that.

Now, you are probably asking "Stacey, how do you know I am loved?" I know just by knowing who created you, *For we are his workmanship, created in Christ Jesus for good works, which God prepared beforehand, that we should walk in them* (Ephesians 2:10).

It's all written right there. You are God's masterpiece – or as David Crowder of the David Crowder Band says: He made everything glorious so what does that make me? It's not conditional because you are in Christ to do good works and by praying boldly above He will show you those works. Once you figure out that somebody loves you no matter what, then you will have no trouble with those good works showing others that **they** are loved too.

And for mercy's sake, stop trying to fit in to a love that doesn't work. How long do you have to struggle with practically begging someone to love you before you realize it doesn't work like that? You are loved from the beginning of time and, if someone chooses not to love you or to treat you badly, I can tell you that is not part of the Big Guy's plan. Don't think for one second that He created you to suffer for love or to suffer for someone else's ego. Your legacy will be the love that you leave behind, not the love you put up with so weigh whatever love you have on earth with the Love that created you.

If you have made it to this part of the book and not accepted the Love talked about in most of these pages, Jesus is waiting. He loves you and He wants to rescue you with a love that is perfect. What are you waiting for? Accept His love today.

Beloved, if God so loved us,
we also ought to love one another.

1 JOHN 4:11

16

JUST GET OUT THERE AND ROLL AROUND A BIT

(Be Happy and Silly)

In my opinion, if you have never eaten jellied beef loaf, you haven't missed anything. In what was Bogey's and still is Johnny's opinion – you haven't lived until you've tried it! Johnny is Swedish, and each trip to his home in Minnesota must include scouring the grocery aisles of several stores for jellied beef loaf. We often find it at a little local store, and he buys every package they have hanging there.

We take it to his mom's and put it in the freezer, leaving one package out to be consumed immediately. Then we pack the rest in our checked luggage and hope it stays frozen for the trip. Most trips, this is not a problem because we are going from one freezing cold climate to another reasonably cold one. Believe me, it was the **first** thing we unpacked when we arrived back in New Jersey. Now that we're in Arizona…well, we'll have to see what happens!

The unpacking always set off a feeding frenzy with Bogey. She would start smelling the suitcase; follow the carrier of the jellied beef loaf to the freezer, watching every step. Once the first package was open, she would dance around on her hind legs until that first piece of bliss hit her mouth (yuck!). She would smack her way through that piece (remember her lack of teeth) while looking for the next.

It's very difficult to describe the look that she would get on her face, but it was one of sheer delight. Her eyes would bug out and her lips would actually form a smile as she panted in anticipation of the next bite. All of this reaction from a dog who refused to beg for anything in her life. But she became the happiest, silliest little dog when the jellied beef loaf was cracked open. She and Johnny would stand in the kitchen, sharing that smelly stuff while I watched with utter amusement. Once Johnny put it back in the fridge, she would follow him around the house for hours with that same look on her face, wondering how she could get him to walk into the kitchen and open up the refrigerator.

I smile even today thinking about how my dignified little dog would melt down to a silly clown when that meat was brought home. If I could help everyone in the world find the one thing that makes them feel that way, I think world peace would be right around the corner.

For me, it is probably purses. My fascination with bags did not come from my mother, who could carry the same purse for years—so it's not genetic. It really is the simple, pure enjoyment that a really great clutch can bring to a girl's life.

And the minute that you admire my purse, look out—it is simply my way of paying it forward to give you whatever bag I have strung over my shoulder. The shampoo girl at my hair salon learned the hard way after I returned with my silver sequin sparkly bag that she casually mentioned matched the sandals she was wearing that day. And that one that my niece loved—I simply traded out for another bag and left it for her birthday.

So maybe it's not the purses but the opportunity to make someone else's day that is my one thing. In radio, you have a lot of chances to have once-in-a-lifetime experiences. But my heart sails when I get to provide someone else with their once-in-a-lifetime. I love to sit back and watch their faces. That is the jellied beef loaf that makes my day.

One time a jellied-beef-loaf-moment turned into a huge opportunity to help our troops. Platinum-selling, Grammy-winning Casting Crowns wanted to have lunch with a group of our listeners. I was contacted by a congregant of a church in Pennsylvania who wanted her pastor and his wife to attend. Their college-age son had collapsed on the soccer field one day and was now mentally challenged. The pastor was in the National Guard and had been sent to Kuwait twice. Their daughter was also a member of the National Guard and had been deployed as well. So Pastor Gary and his wife, Lois, came to lunch.

Being my human self, I thought that was the end of the story. They enjoyed their time with the band and then went to the concert that night and were further blessed. But God had bigger plans for this once-in-a-lifetime. During the conversation over lunch, Mark Hall, Casting Crown's lead singer, mentioned to Pastor Gary that he had always wanted to go entertain the troops but had never had the opportunity. That set the wheels in motion, and eight months later Casting Crowns performed for some of the biggest crowds of troops to ever attend a concert in Kuwait.

I have so many stories like that, where my little once-in-a-lifetime for someone else turned into something God-huge because I found my delight in other people's joy. And, by the way, with a November birthday, if you ever give me a gift card, I will use it to buy something for someone else. That's a fair warning; I just can't help myself.

But back to "happy silliness." A lot of Christians think that you always have to be serious and somber to follow Christ. I couldn't disagree with them more because God created our sense of humor and wants us to use it to help others. The person without a smile is the first person that I can reach for Christ because He gives us so much to smile about. I often picture Him walking down the road with His apostles and laughing about something silly one of them had said or done.

Our happy silliness is something people can't understand when it is so hard to live in today's world. They struggle through, never finding their jellied beef loaf and wonder what it is that we have to be so happy about. I can tell you the number one thing to be happy about is that Jesus loves us enough to give His life for us so that we can experience the freedom of happiness. Even if I were the only person on earth, Jesus would have still given His life for me. I smile at the thought.

Our happy silliness is something people can't understand when it is so hard to live in today's world.

I mentioned before that Johnny's office was downstairs in our New Jersey home. If we were on different levels for an extended period of time, he would yell up "Love!" In return, I simply responded with "Love!" then we went on with our days. That reassurance of our happiness and love has kept us going through the toughest times. Yes, some of you might call it silly, but we call it love.

Women are often running around, trying to find a man who will throw down their coat for them in some grand expression of love when life's mud puddles are all around. But all they have to do is have faith that Jesus did so much more for them and has planned a grand love for them that can't be matched by the missing jacket man. There is no greater love than that of a friend who is willing to surrender his or her life for another (see John 15:13). Well, you already have a friend that has done that, and His name is Jesus.

Toward the end of her life, my grandmother stopped going to the hair salon to get her fake toenails put on. Yes, she had to have them to wear her sandals. So I became Stacey the manicurist and regularly did her fingernails and toenails.

I was busy one afternoon, cleaning the gunk out from under her toenails, when I must have had a very serious look on my face. It was pretty stinky job as I recall, so maybe that was it. She pulled my face up by the chin, and said, "Stacey, be happy."

I simply smiled and went on with my scraping, but that moment stuck with me. Our silly happiness is a choice, and I choose today to smile at the jellied-beef moments.

For you shall go out in joy
and be led forth in peace;
the mountains and the hills before you
shall break forth into singing,
and all the trees of the field
shall clap their hands.

ISAIAH 55:12

Johnny

We had some very cool moments while we were in the New York Metro. From Radio City Music Hall to a prayer service in Times Square, God gave us these times to remember for a long, long time.

One particularly awesome morning came when we were invited by NBC to broadcast from the Amy Grant performance at Rockefeller Center. The four of us plus a few promotions folks caravanned to the middle of Manhattan and found a parking garage where all of the NBC execs had their parking spaces. (Don't worry David. I won't mention how you ran the STAR van into a pole on that trip).

Lugging all of our equipment up to the second floor of the NBC store, we had a bird's eye view of the performance and a pretty cool opportunity to describe it for everyone listening. If you have never been to Rockefeller Center, it looks quite a bit bigger on television. And the crowds were packed in there to see Amy along with the Today Show crew. Everything went without a hitch as we broadcast and we played Bible Or Not and Beat The Toaster from that location.

At the end of the show, each of the four of us; me, Stacey, Dawn and David, told what we had going on that day or what we were thankful for or amazed by. I don't know if it was because Stacey didn't sleep well the night before or the excitement of the morning but for some strange reason Stacey started talking about the toenail clippers she bought on QVC the week before. She went on to extol the virtues of these fantastic clippers and we were all just staring at her like she had lost her mind. The mics shut off and everyone around the table, including the NBC security guards just burst out laughing. It was truly in that second that we could not stop guffawing and were so happy to be a small part of God's great universe.

17

Howl if You Need To

(Let It Out)

One day I went to the vet to pick up shampoo for Mally. It had been almost a year since I was there with Bogey when she took her final breaths. I had (I thought) worked through the pain of returning to that office. And I just had to pick up shampoo; I didn't even have to go into the room where Bogey laid on her little bed looking up at me, so I thought I was good to go.

Then a woman who looked like she had been up for days walked around the corner with an empty cat carrier. She was visibly shaken and needed to leave, but she had to pay her bill first and ended up right behind me at the counter. Looking down at the carrier and back at her tear-stained face, I knew that I was looking back into the past of my suffering. The receptionist finished with me and quickly went over to check the woman out so that her pain could exit the building with her.

As I walked out, I put my hand on that woman's shoulder and said, "May God bless you and keep you." She simply replied, "Thank you." With tears streaming down my face, I walked out the same path I had taken with an empty blanket gripped in my arms eleven months earlier. I got into the car and cried, thinking that we never know when the hole in our hearts will open up, and we will love someone because she is going through what we went through, and we understand.

I read a report recently that said most people move past abject grief six months after their loss. But I think there are some losses you never get past. Let me give you permission to believe the same thing if you need to. Even Jesus grieved with Mary and Martha over Lazarus when He knew He was going to raise Lazarus from the dead. He felt their pain and anguish so strongly even while He knew the happy ending that was coming. Jesus grieves because we suffer loss, and He provides comfort even when we don't recognize it.

Even Jesus grieved with Mary and Martha over Lazarus when He knew He was going to raise Lazarus from the dead.

When I moved to New Jersey, I had a mouth full of rotten teeth. Nice, huh? Well, I had been taking care of my grandmother for months and not my teeth, so the moment I got insurance, I went straight to the dentist. Four cavities and two root canals/crowns later, I was sitting in the lobby of the dentist's building waiting for my ride.

Suddenly the cold air rushed in as a businesswoman blew through the doors. She was looking at her cell phone and carrying her day planner as she quickly entered the building. Suddenly she stopped dead in her tracks in front of me. With a gasp, she asked me if I was all right. I mumbled something unintelligible because of the anesthesia, and she sat down next to me. She chatted while I somehow grunted out my life story. When my ride arrived, she went on her way to the elevator, never to be seen by me again.

In that moment, she was what I **needed** to survive the wait. She also gave me the hope that everything that was said about people in New Jersey was not true. Maybe she was an angel, but whoever she was, she was kind, and that was what I needed. Whatever you are going through right now, I guarantee there is someone who cares and would sit with you on the bench for a while.

But you have to realize you will also be called to sit with someone later on who is suffering as you suffer now. That is the way life works, and maybe the knowledge you are gaining in your pain will be the lifeline someone will need to survive.

I took a course on grief in college, and I do believe that Dr. Kubler-Ross's five stages of grief (Denial, Anger, Bargaining, Depression, and Acceptance) apply in many different situations. People start and stop the stages as individuals, and they revert back to them as they continue to live. So how can anyone tell you that it is time for you to be done with your grief? That leads to you keeping it all inside, not knowing how wonderful you can feel when it all comes flowing out.

You have to live in this crazy world where you are expected to achieve healing in three months or less and get on with your life after two weeks off if you have lost a close family member. I am here to tell you to cry at your desk. Oh, no! I didn't just say that. Oh, yes, I did! The world will not tilt off of its axis if you are grieving when you are supposed to be working. Let it out. Let it all out.

Now, realize where the edge is. This is about you and dealing with what you are going through. So the minute you feel like taking a baseball bat to something or someone, get help. But don't subscribe to the world's belief that you are supposed to be better by now. Ecclesiastes 3:4 lets you off the hook when it says there is a time to weep, and a time to laugh; a time to mourn, and a time to dance. It's not just a song, you know.

When Jesus was here on earth, so many people turned to him in their hour of greatest need. For instance, in Matthew 8:8 a powerful centurion came to Jesus and asked for help for his paralyzed servant – Lord, I am not worthy to have you come under my roof, but only say the word, and my servant will be healed. Was it so easy for this man of power and rank to stand in faith in front of Jesus and ask for healing for one of his servants? And now, in our greatest hour of need and grief, we don't even have to face Him but simply believe that He exists and ask for His help.

How do you know when you receive His help? I pray that there are times in your life when you ask to see Him and He shows you what He can do. One Sunday after church, Johnny and I were headed down the FDR (Franklin D. Roosevelt) highway, and Johnny was surfing the car radio channels the way any radio geek would. He was actually working when he should have been enjoying the drive, but that is another point for another book! He landed on a local channel that was playing Lonestar's song I'm Already There. He immediately starts to change the channel, but I grab his hand and stop him. Then he pleads with me not to start crying. "I won't cry if you don't change the channel," I promised. You see, that song means a great deal to me because of my nieces Deven and Layne, and I hadn't heard it in three years. When I moved to Chicago, that song was very popular and the words really hit home. I would call my nieces or e-mail them whenever it came on. When they came to visit me and it would come on the radio, they would laugh at their silly aunt who was crying over a song. It took me quite a few years not to cry when I heard that song. So that Sunday, I sang along, "I'm already there. Take a look around – I'm the sunshine in your hair, I'm the shadow on the ground." I sang without crying and I thought of all of the happy times we had together.

The reason we were driving down the FDR that Sunday was because we had read reports of all of the development at Ground Zero but had never seen it for ourselves. It was amazing to see how tall the Freedom Tower and other buildings were getting to be! Johnny stepped out of the car to take a picture, and I suddenly realized that the last time I was at Ground Zero, there was snow on the ground, and Layne had been with me.

I picked up my cell phone to text Layne to tell her that I

loved her, and a text from my mother popped up. I sat there with my mouth agape because the text was about Layne. She had fallen the day before while holding her one-year-old daughter. The child was fine, but Layne had broken her left tibia. I calmly called Layne, and we reminisced about our trip to Ground Zero and she told me all about her accident. The most fascinating part of this story is that Layne lives in San Diego with her husband and baby. My mother sent me the text from Dallas, and there I was sitting at Ground Zero in NYC. God's plan was perfectly orchestrated. Do I think songs come on the radio for a reason? I think there are no coincidences with God—even in the little things that happen to us. We just need to see God in them.

Let me tell you, when you are going through a tragedy or recovering from a loss, God will use anything to get through to you. I can't tell you how many times we hear the stories of people whose lives were saved because the right song came on at just the right time. Remember the story of the teenager who was going to kill himself until his CD player wouldn't work and his radio would pick up only one Christian station playing the song that saved his life?

Let me tell you, when you are going through a tragedy or recovering from a loss, God will use anything to get through to you.

Another story is of an elderly man who starts to walk out the back door with a shotgun to take his life and, every time he picks it up, he hears the same song on the radio. It doesn't matter if it is night or day when he attempts to kill himself, the same song comes on and stops him in his tracks. He ends up mailing the shotgun shell to the local radio station because he just can't do it. This is not coincidence; this is God. You can tell God about your pain and let him handle it.

If you wake up one morning and your radio will pick up only one station, pay attention. God may be trying to tell you something. One day he was trying to tell me something, and I was too embattled in my grief to hear him. It was the Sunday after Thanksgiving 2008, and I had been suffering from terrible chest pains for months. No medications would help, and no tests would tell me was what going on, but I ended up in the emergency room a couple of times because the pain was so great. Johnny and I were driving down the Garden State Parkway (we seem to be driving a lot in these stories!) and my phone rang. It was a private number, so I decide I had better answer it. When I did, my doctor is on the other end, saying that he knows what is wrong with me. It seems that I have entered menopause way early, and they can help me with that, but I will never be able to have children.

The tears started to flow as this overachiever who had to get two degrees and be successful in her field just wanted to go back about ten years and have a baby. It wasn't that my life was built around my becoming a mother. It was just that it was always a possibility, and now it was no more. Through my tears I declared to Johnny that I didn't care what happened or what changed, but I was never going to church on Mother's Day ever again. I think I may have even said something really crude about those carnations they hand out and where they could put them (remember, I was in pain!).

So we went through the grief process over the child that we were never going to have, and we invested a little more deeply in the fur babies we had at the moment. I went on with my career and kept striving to serve God more every day.

Then one day I got an e-mail from my pastor asking for my opinion on something that he and another pastor were planning to teach on. I sent back a detailed e-mail, and they thanked me. A couple of days later, the pastor asked if I would be willing to be a guest speaker on the topic. Oh, it gets better because guess what day they want me to join them onstage? Mother's Day! I told him I would pray about it and get back to him. Then I threw myself down on the floor and shook my fist at the sky and wondered what in the world God was up to. But

I knew he was up to something, so I agreed to do it. Suddenly I was not only going to church on Mothers' Day; I was going to four services to speak, and there was to be a baby dedication at one of them! But I delighted in preparing my message, and I began to see the opportunity to speak on Mothers' Day as a gift from God.

Johnny was very supportive and knew what this meant to me, so off we went to church that Mother's Day. I arrived early, had a quick run-through of the service and a sound check, and prayed with the staff. As I sat in a little corner of the hallway to pray and to review my notes, I heard the parents and their other children coming down the hall for the baby dedication. I got up and stood there staring at the families as they went by. I felt like shrinking into the floor, when suddenly I sensed a strong presence speaking directly to me: "You can't reach as many children for me if you have a child of your own." I shook my head, and realizing my humanness, He said it again. I leaned back against the wall and thought about what had just happened. All of my grief over my never-to-be child had a purpose in Him. Just like in Genesis 50:20, *As for you, you meant evil against me, but God meant it for good, to bring it about that many people should be kept alive, as they are today.*

I have preached many times since then across this country (including Mother's Day several times) and whatever I thought was meant to harm me, God

Ask God to show you today what purpose there is for your grief, and then promise Him that you will be listening.

has used for good. Ask God to show you today what purpose there is for your grief, and then promise Him that you will be listening. Then listen!

For everything there is a season,
and a time for every matter under heaven:
a time to be born, and a time to die;
a time to plant, and a time to pluck up what is planted;
a time to kill, and a time to heal;
a time to break down, and a time to build up;
a time to weep, and a time to laugh;
a time to mourn, and a time to dance.

Ecclesiastes 3:1-4

Johnny

It really seems funny now that the little dog that crawled into my heart and cleaned out my savings account was such an irritant to begin with. I'll never forget the day that she left us. I left Stacey at home with her to grieve, tell her stories and wait but the show contained a topic that I had no idea was God chosen. David, Dawn and I talked about what makes a best friend. We took hundreds of calls on what each person thought made a best friend until the hotline in the studio started ringing.

Dawn picked up the phone and it was Stacey on the other end. You could hear the cry voice and sniffles as I picked up the phone, worried that Bogey had gone on without us and Stacey was left there with her alone. But in her weak little voice filled with grief Stacey said, "I just wanted to tell you what makes a best friend." I had no idea that she had even been listening so I said "okay". Then she cleared her throat and said "A best friend is someone who will go with me this afternoon to say goodbye to my precious little dog."

There was not a dry eye in the studio as we hung up the phone. And now there is not a dry eye here as I think about that time and what it meant for us to walk through that together. Stacey was right, being a best friend sometimes means having to bear the grief of someone you love.

18

Unleashed at Last

(The Clarity of Our Faith)

ight after Johnny and I got married, I moved into the townhouse that he had purchased several months back. At first I thought I was losing my eyesight, which is nothing to joke about, but then I realized that it was just really, really dark inside this place! It seems when the home was built, it did not come with built in lighting so, once everything settled down a bit, we went in search of illumination for our new home.

We traveled over to Irvington, NJ to a large (that's an understatement) warehouse that sold nothing but lighting. They had $60,000 chandeliers and $5 lamps (those were the ones we were looking for). It was lighting for miles and miles so we set off separately to find two or three light fixtures that we each liked and then show them to the other person. I had my neck craned back looking at a ceiling fan with a light when I heard a huge crash from a few aisles over. My heart sank with the thought that somehow Johnny had been part of that crash. I walked slowly over to the aisle where the crash had come from and leaned over to see Johnny and the sales woman bent over a broken lamp. They were both talking very fast so I took my sweet time getting any closer thinking that all of the "you break it, you bought it" signs suddenly applied to our checkbook.

But once I got closer, I noticed something very different. It became very clear that it was not Johnny who had broken the lamp but the sales lady. She was visibly upset so Johnny was trying to help her pick it up and put some of the parts back together. While we were assisting her, she said "I'll be right back" and left us with this beautiful Tiffany replication standing on the desk beside us in pieces. We kinda shrugged and went off in search of our own fixtures. Johnny explained that she was trying to sell the lamp to him when she grabbed one of the inside features and it came off in her hand. The rest starting falling off and neither one could stop the crashing pieces. I showed Johnny a few of the fixtures that I had picked out when the sales lady involved in the lamp incident came around the corner. She asked Johnny, "Do you want to buy that lamp?" We both just looked at each other because that lamp in its original condition would have totally broken our budget. The sales woman must have seen our distress because she quickly added, "I'll sell it to you for $50."

Yes, we bought the lamp. Johnny totally rewired it to make it safe and today we have a beautiful Tiffany replica in our bedroom. But my original pessimistic confusion shines brightly in each bulb of that lamp. My mind automatically jumped to the worst possible scene when I heard the crash at the lighting store.

The same thing happened when Johnny and I took our first trip as a married couple. We decided that we were going to Washington, D.C. to see the Fourth of July fireworks. It was just a quick weekend trip so we decided that Bogey could come along. The Watergate Hotel allowed dogs at that time so we decided to stay at the historic hotel. It was a wonderful trip but the temperature was in the upper 90's the entire time.

To say that the heat affected our trip would be another

understatement. I ended up carrying Bogey for most of the first day because the street and sidewalks were entirely too hot for her little paws. Oh, and she let you know it was too hot with a whine and a look that said "You brought me into this situation, you are going to carry me out!" My arms were cramping and my assumption was that the day was pretty much a bust because neither one of us could go much farther. That's when my superhero of a husband kicked into gear (for the first time that day). Johnny looked at both Bogey and I and said, "I'll be right back." He rushed into a drug store and came out with an umbrella stroller. The minute he opened it, I put Bogey in and she did not move for the rest of the day.

We went and saw all of the attractions, walked down the Mall and went into restaurants with this precious little dog in that stroller. The day that I saw as lost was turned wonderful until the heat caused me to have a migraine. There are wonderful pictures of us strolling the little dog around and then there is one with her sleeping beside me on top of the bed while I suffer with a headache. The fireworks that we had worked so hard to see were out of the question.

That is, until my husband decided to play superhero one more time that day. I did not even hear him leave but I heard his return. "I went and talked to the concierge," Johnny explained. He had talked the hotel staff into letting us go up on the top of the Watergate Hotel to a private party and watch the fireworks. I barely made it to the roof but we watched the fireworks from a corner of the party knowing if we acted like we were supposed to be there, no one would say anything. Two major obstacles in one day and two major solutions, even when I thought all was lost.

There is always a way to change your situation or view things from a different perspective.

There is always a way to change your situation or view things from a different perspective. Maybe that clarity comes with age or maybe from being married to Johnny.

But the most important question for today is "How do you see your faith?" Are you like me, Debbie Downer, who always sees obstacles and roadblocks to being still and knowing He is God? Are you hoping that someday you will build up enough faith to tell others about the saving love of Jesus Christ? God has given us a tremendous gift of clarity in our faith if we will only search out and recognize it.

In Hebrews 11:1, God breaks it down for us so we can celebrate that clarity. In the very first word, He informs us of **when** we should have faith—and that would be NOW! He doesn't start out with "when" or "how" – He starts out with **now** and sets up a challenge for all of us that believe and those that will someday; start believing now! He moves on by saying, "Now faith is confidence..." and confidence is a state where most of us thrive. If you can find within your belief the confidence that builds upon the foundation of our Cornerstone, you will have no problem with the rest of this verse. We teach children confidence and striving all throughout their lives and there are theorists that believe the main goal or push of humans is to live in confidence. For us the confidence in what we hope for is everything and allows us to encounter the significance of believing in God.

> **He informs us of when we should have faith—and that would be NOW!**

Hope stands as a descriptive of what we believe. I was hoping that Johnny had nothing to do with the lamp fiasco and I was desperately hoping for relief from the heat in D.C. The Hope that we have in Jesus Christ goes way beyond earthly hope and can take away many of the struggles we face if we let it. Conversely, what you are hoping for leads the way to where you are going. You make the choice of what type of hope to hold onto, so today may I suggest you review your hopes and choose the ones that bring you closer Christ.

Then there is assurance. Some people, who have no understanding of our faith, believe assurance is the farthest thing from what we are feeling but they don't fully understand how our God works. See, the definition of assurance is "a positive declaration intended to give confidence." Oh yes, He just did! He took our confidence from earlier in the verse and turned it around for us to see. The assurance of what we do not see is simply the outward spoken word of confidence that tells the world of our faith. I once heard a pastor teach that we are the symphony of Jesus to a world who desperately needs to hear it. It takes confidence to play that symphony and our assurances of what we cannot see put the notes together in fine fashion.

So in one little verse God takes our faith and wraps in up in the beautiful package of clarity. He knows we can peak around the corner and see who broke the lamp. He also knows we can have the faith to know He is around that corner cleaning up our messes. If you lack clarity in your faith today, look back at His promises. He has kept His end of the bargain!

Now faith is the assurance of things hoped for, the conviction of things not seen.

HEBREWS 11:1

19

YOUR FOREVER HOME

(Our Breed Is Rescued)

*I*f you have read this far and not figured out that Jesus is the Ultimate Rescuer, this chapter is for you.

When you think of a rescue dog, you probably think of lines of cages with dogs looking through the fence holes at you, a sense of hopelessness in their gaze as they know that you may be their last chance for a forever home. It has been years since I have walked into an animal shelter because I cannot take the pain. I would release all of them into my neighbor's yards if I had the chance; so instead I pray for those who take care of these dogs and the families that adopt each precious one.

My brother, Jimmy, loves dogs, and my nieces, when they were much younger, thought he needed a new playmate. They show up for his birthday with a Dalmatian that they named Princess; I am pretty sure that my brother did none of the naming. Then the two little girls decided that Princess needed a friend, so they went and picked out a Basset Hound. I think Jimmy may have been part of that naming because they called him Humphrey.

Those two dogs were truly rescued because they were in a kill shelter, and they both lived tremendous lives filled with love, joy, and lots of treats. But on a July day in Texas in 2009, my brother called me on the phone hysterical. I was walking to Central Park, and my first thought was something had happened to one of my parents or my nieces. He could not get out what was wrong, so I panicked until he yelled into the phone, "Humphrey's dead!" At age fourteen, Humphrey could not make it through another hot Texas summer. Unfortunately, he had hidden himself in the bushes to die so Jimmy could do nothing but kneel on the ground next to him and cry. I listened for a long time while Jimmy blamed himself for not taking good enough care of him, keeping him outside for his entire life, not keeping the cable guy out of the backyard, on and on and on. In his grief, he needed answers as to why this had happened.

But there were no answers. Bad things happen to good dog owners. No one was at home with him, so I called around until I found family members to go help with getting Humphrey out of the bushes and his body disposed of. I was relieved Jimmy had called me and I had been able to answer the phone that day.

There is a Rescuer who is always on call and always with us. He was with Jimmy that day when he couldn't find Humphrey and came across his lifeless body. He is with you when you are in the ICU with your loved one and the doctors have no answers. He is with you when the worst possible thing that could happen is taking place. Jesus is with you and promises to never leave you.

Jesus is with you and promises to never leave you.

But you have to accept it and begin a personal relationship with Him. We all try to do it on our own; it's the American way! There is not a day that goes by that I don't struggle with staying on the path that leads to peace and comfort by trusting

He wants what is best for me. Admitting we have sinned and fallen short of the glory of God is a tough thing. But if you have told a little white lie or simply hidden something (including purchases) from your spouse in the past week, guess what? My sins have gone way past those, so don't worry. God takes our sins and casts them into the deepest ocean. Psalm 103:12 tells us that *as far as the east is from the west, so far does he remove our transgressions from us.* In fact, **we** are the only ones who keep bringing them up because He forgives us much better than we forgive ourselves.

If you look at this book as a list of the blessings in my life, you are right on the money. When I decided to lay down my life and follow Him, my life changed. You have to speak directly to God, tell Him that you have sinned, that you are sorry, and that you want Jesus to be your personal Savior. Then listen because God has a plan for you.

In the hymn titled, ***He Lives***, it says, "He walks with me and talks with me, along life's narrow way." There is something to those words, and once you give your life to Him, He will talk to you in four different ways. Bill Hybels, in his book *Too Busy to Pray,* points out three ways (but I have to add a fourth). When you are listening and ready to accept what God has planned for you, he will speak directly to you through His Word, other people, gentle nudges—and music. The Bible is the ultimate self-help book, and praying that God will lead you to the right verse or passage to study is always helpful. Never spend a day without reading what God has to say about how to live your life and how to treat others.

The godly people in your life know what you are going through and can speak directly into your situation if they are in the Word and have your best interest at heart. I pray you have someone like this to whom you can turn, someone who can hold you accountable. When such a person says something, evaluate what he or she is saying against what God says in the Bible, and go with it if it does not contradict God's Word. You must have discernment when it comes to listening to others or when God nudges you to do something. God never sends someone to tell you something that is completely against His teachings, and He will never nudge you to sin. It's just that simple. Don't start with the justifications when it is something you want and God never had a hand in it. That's bad news, my friend.

And then there is music. I cannot tell you how many times I have heard someone tell a story about hearing the right song at just the right time on our radio station. During one fundraiser, a dad called to tell the story of his son who was trying to commit suicide. The young man went into the woods in his car, attached a hose to the muffler, and put it through the window. He had planned to end his life listening to a heavy metal CD. When he put the CD into the radio, it spit it right back out. He tried several times and could not get the radio to play the CD. So he turned on the radio, scanning up and down the dial for heavy metal music, but the only station it would land on was STAR. You might be thinking this was a coincidence, but "Cry Out To Jesus" by Third Day was playing, and the young man pushed the hose out the window and follows Jesus to this day. This is just one true story out of hundreds that I have heard with my own ears. You may want to listen a little more closely to the words of the songs next time you turn on the radio.

How does God call out to you? Each person's experience is different, but I want to make sure you are listening. I was there when Jimmy called. Are you going to call out to God, or be listening when God calls out to you?

It's so funny because when people used to ask me what breed my dogs were, I would say "They're just mutts." Then I would wince because we are all just mutts in some way. So now I proudly say, "Our breed is rescued!" because I have been rescued by Jesus more times than I can count!

*Because he inclined his ear to me, therefore
I will call on him as long as I live.*

PSALM 116:2

FIND A GOOD HOME

(There's a New Sheriff In Town)

"Why don't we go look at the fur babies up for adoption?" Oh, he knew better but Johnny made the suggestion anyway and, after I protested a little bit, off we went to see what cuteness awaited us. Now, let me back up for a moment because we just went to the pet food store for dog food for Mally and had no plan to even look at the precious little faces in the cages that day. When Johnny paused at the big dog cage to look at a few bulldogs that were available I traveled on around the corner to the little dog area. I turned the corner around stacks of pet products and there he was! Sweet black and white face stretched over the floor cage with a look that said "Where have you been?!?!?"

I know there were signs saying "Don't touch the dogs!" and "Don't reach into the cage!" but all I saw was this precious little one and all he saw was me. I picked him up, looked him in the face and he collapsed onto my chest curling his little head into the crook of my neck. Johnny describes that moment as him coming around the corner to find me looking up at him with the big cartoon hearts shooting out of my eyes. He was

137

a Jack Russell terrier mix that weighed about 9 pounds and his head was entirely too big for his body. The woman at the adoption center called him Baxter but that would never do. It was already a done deal but we still had to talk Johnny into the arrangement so I had to put him back in the cage where he bounced back up on his hind legs looking at me with those "Where are you going?" eyes.

It didn't take long and we had a new sheriff in town! Ringo came home with us that day and brings new joy to Johnny, Mally and me each day. (Well, Mally most days.) That is one thing that I have learned is that life goes on. Our little pack lives in Tucson now, hence his cowboy name, and God's blessings have followed us here. So many more stories, perhaps another entire book worth, but each highlights a different promise that God has kept. And that is my prayer for you as you hold these final pages; that something that I said connected to bring you hope and that you stubbornly don't give up when all seems wrong.

God told me to write this book for you. So many people have stood in opposition to it's publication but when all of it is said and done, they were not doubting me but doubting Him. You now get to decide what you do with what it taught and I know you will make the right decision. You don't want to miss the joy before the sadness and the joy after the sadness.

Stay Blessed,

Stacey

CONNECT

Connect with other fans and share your own stories at
www.Facebook.com/TheRescuedBreed

Check out
www.TheRescuedBreed.com
where you can download additional resources and bonus
materials only available on the website.

You can also order additional copies of the book for
your friends and family, and get information on how to
have Stacey speak at your next gathering.

Stacey would love to hear from you! Connect via email at
Stacey@TheRescuedBreed.com

You can also follow Stacey on social media:

- *www.Facebook.com/StaceyStone*
- *www.Facebook.com/JohnnyandStaceyStone*
- *www.Twitter.com/StaceyStone (@StaceyStone)*